a Spiritual Journey to GOD'S BEST

a Spiritual Journey to
GOD'S BEST

40 LESSONS REVEALED
FEAR to FAITH

*by Understanding the
Relationship Between God,
Jesus, the Holy Spirit & You*

MICHAELYN HODGES

NASHVILLE

NEW YORK • MELBOURNE • VANCOUVER

a *Spiritual Journey* to GOD'S BEST
40 LESSONS REVEALED
FEAR *to* FAITH *by Understanding the Relationship Between*
God, Jesus, the Holy Spirit & You

Published in New York, New York, by Morgan James Publishing. Morgan James and The Entrepreneurial Publisher are trademarks of Morgan James, LLC.
www.MorganJamesPublishing.com

The Morgan James Speakers Group can bring authors to your live event. For more information or to book an event visit The Morgan James Speakers Group at
www.TheMorganJamesSpeakersGroup.com.

Shelfie

A **free** eBook edition is available
with the purchase of this print book.

CLEARLY PRINT YOUR NAME ABOVE IN UPPER CASE

Instructions to claim your free eBook edition:
1. Download the Shelfie app for Android or iOS
2. Write your name in **UPPER CASE** above
3. Use the Shelfie app to submit a photo
4. Download your eBook to any device

ISBN 978-1-68350-337-8 paperback
ISBN 978-1-68350-338-5 eBook
ISBN 978-1-68350-339-2 hardcover
Library of Congress Control Number:
2016918453

Cover Design by:
Rachel Lopez
www.r2cdesign.com

Interior Design by:
Bonnie Bushman
The Whole Caboodle Graphic Design

In an effort to support local communities, raise awareness and funds, Morgan James Publishing donates a percentage of all book sales for the life of each book to Habitat for Humanity Peninsula and Greater Williamsburg.

Get involved today! Visit
www.MorganJamesBuilds.com

DEDICATIONS

This book is dedicated to the reader
and whatever you are going through.

May the information in this book be for you the well dug
that God fills from the top with His holy waters. God is
with you and will never leave you or forsake you.

To my husband, whom I love with all my heart. And to my
children, Cole and Katie, I love you and thank you for putting up
with my imperfectness. Always do everything to the glory of God.

TABLE OF CONTENTS

Acknowledgments

Many thanks to my family and friends who supported and prayed for me and helped me move this book forward, Christine, Roberta, Jerrilea, Alexandra, Terri, Suzanne, Teresa, Senayet, Brenda, Jan, Kelly, Janis, the faithful ladies of the "Red Church", Dianne McDermott for her paintings, and a special thanks to my editor, Barbara Hollace, whose mentoring and editing helped make this book my best for God.

PRELUDE

To receive the Word of God, we must persevere as we seek the truth. The truth will set us free. The strongholds in my life kept me in bondage, but I was set free by learning and understanding the truth of God's Word. Jesus sought me when I was living a life of sin. He continues to convict me and patiently shows me through the Holy Spirit, the areas where I need to change. Now I have hope of an eternal future with Him.

When God created me, He gave me the desire to thoroughly study a concept until I finally get it. I was the annoying one who always raised her hand in class. He also gave me the gift of discernment and the ability to understand that I am to pay attention when He is teaching me something. God uses the weak and the unlikely. I think that's why He chose me, someone with a degree in Horticulture and limited writing skills, to write this book. What I did learn in college is to get right to the point. God told me that He is going to use the lessons I have learned like a well dug by a pilgrim that He takes and fills from the top with His holy water, or Holy Spirit. His message encouraged me to keep learning and to keep writing even though I felt condemnation for not being a Bible scholar. It has taken me seven years to put this book together and two decades of going through the fire to learn these lessons. Praise God if it can be a little speedier for you.

God revealed to me that He was going to use this book on September 12, 2012. I heard the Holy Spirit tell me to find Charles Spurgeon's devotional (revised by Alistair Begg) "Morning and Evening" that was in my dresser drawer that hadn't been opened for at least a year and read that day's passage. I was on my way out the door to take my children to school and didn't have time. About two o'clock I heard the Holy Spirit repeat that I was to look at today's message in the devotional. When I opened the book, this is what I found. "Travelers have been delighted to see the footprint of man on a barren shore, and we love to see the marks of pilgrims while passing through the vale of tears. The pilgrims dig the well, but, strangely, it fills from the top instead of the bottom. We use the means, but the blessing does not spring from the means. We dig a well, but heaven fills it with rain."

My prayer is that God will speak to you, the reader, through the Holy Spirit and these lessons will help you on your own journey. There will be resistance from the enemy as you read this book, so keep persevering, it will be worth it. May God bless you and send His angels to watch over you.

Michaelyn Hodges

(Maikəlin)

Introduction to Week 1

SEEKING THE TRUTH

In the verses below, Jesus is telling us to seek the truth of His Word. He came to this world to reveal the truth to us. Seek His truth with all your heart by diligently studying His Word, which is the seed, so that it may be planted in good soil and take root. Persevere by reading and understanding His Word as you go through life's trials and reap the harvest of blessings that He has in store for you.

Heavenly Father, I pray that You will speak to me through Your Word and provide divine understanding of Your truth. Give me ears to hear and eyes to see and a heart to understand. In Jesus' name I pray, amen.

And he said to them, "Do you not understand this parable? How then will you understand all the parables? The sower sows the word. And these are the ones along the path, where the word is sown: when they hear, Satan immediately comes and takes away the word that is sown in them. And these are the ones sown on rocky ground: the ones who, when they hear the word, immediately receive it with joy. And they have no root in themselves, but endure for a while; then, when tribulation or persecution arises on account of the word, immediately they fall away. And others are the ones sown among thorns. They are those who hear the word, but the cares of the world and the deceitfulness of riches and the desires for other things enter in and choke the word, and it proves unfruitful. But those that were sown on the good soil are the ones who hear the word and accept it and bear fruit, thirtyfold and sixtyfold and a hundredfold." Mark 4:13–20 (ESV)

For as the rain comes down, and the snow from heaven, and do not return there, but water the earth, and make it bring forth and bud, that it may give seed to the sower and bread to the eater, so shall My word be that goes forth from My mouth; it shall not return to Me void, But I shall accomplish what I please, and it shall prosper in the thing for which I sent it. Isaiah 55:10–11 (NKJV)

So Jesus said to the Jews who had believed him, "If you abide in my word, you are truly my disciples, and you will know the truth, and the truth will set you free." John 8:31–32 (ESV)

"You are king, then!" said Pilate. Jesus answered, "You are right in saying I am a king. In fact, for this reason I was born, and for this reason I came into the world, to testify to the truth. Everyone on the side of truth listens to me." John 18:37

We should begin this journey by eliminating things in our lives that prevent us from growing closer to God. It has become common to walk into a store and see a variety of statues of false gods. They are often seen in a garden or on a shelf in someone's home. Two examples would be a Buddha statue or an Indian fertility carving. If you have any false idols that you are knowingly or unknowingly worshipping, now is the time to get rid of them. The Bible tells us that God's blessings for us are withheld when we worship idols. God is jealous for us. He says to love Me "with all your heart and with all your soul and with all your strength" (Deuteronomy 6:5) and "have no other gods before Me." (Exodus 20:3)

"And there is no God apart from me, a righteous God and a Savior; there is none but me." Isaiah 45:21b

Those who cling to worthless idols forfeit the grace that could be theirs. Jonah 2:8

"I am the Lord your God, who brought you out of the land of Egypt, out of the house of slavery. You shall have no other gods before me. You shall not make for yourself a carved image, or any likeness of anything that is in heaven above, or that is in the earth beneath, or that is in the water under the earth. You shall not bow down to them or serve them, for I the Lord your God am a jealous God, visiting the iniquity of the fathers on the children to the third and the fourth generation of those who hate me, but showing steadfast love to thousands of those who love me and keep my commandments."
Exodus 20:2–6 (ESV)

Be careful, or you will be enticed to turn away and worship other gods and bow down to them. Then the LORD'S anger will burn against you, and He will shut the heavens so that it will not rain and the ground will yield no produce, and you will soon perish from the good land the LORD is giving you. Fix these words of mine in your hearts and minds; tie them as symbols on your hands and bind them on your foreheads.
Deuteronomy 11:16–18

Suggestion for Group Bible Study

Together read the "Prelude" and "Introduction: Seeking His Truth" and answer the Group Questions and Discussion. Review the "Quick Reference Prayers" at the end of the book. Then read Lesson 1: "Where Does Fear Come From?" out loud. Pray for one another to stay on course to finish this study together. Perhaps assign a buddy and share contact info to help encourage one another each week.

For the next 10 weeks, as a group, begin in prayer and then review the lessons from the past week and answer the group questions. If possible, play one or two of the suggested songs from the past week with a cell phone and a Bluetooth speaker. Next, read together the first lesson of the following week, individually answer the questions for this lesson and then pray for one another. The rest of the lessons for the week can be done at home or with your buddy.

FIRST DAY
GROUP QUESTIONS

According to the above passage of Mark 4:13–20

1. What does the seed represent? (Reference Luke 8:11)

2. Which best represents the condition of your heart? (Reference Luke 8:15)

3. Who can come and take the word away from you on the path?

4. What does the rocky soil represent?

5. What chokes out the word in the thorny soil?

6. How do we plant the word in good soil and have it take root?

7. What kind of harvest does God promise us in His Word?

(Isaiah 55:11) God's Word never returns _____

(John 8:32) What will set us free?

(John 18:37) Why did Jesus come into the world?

(Jonah 2:8) Those who cling to _____ _____ *forfeit the grace that could be theirs.*

(Isaiah 45:21b) "And there is no God apart from _____, *a righteous God and Savior; there is none but me."*

(Exodus 20:2–6) You shall not bow down to them or serve them, for I the Lord God am a _____ *God.*

GROUP DISCUSSION

1. *Discuss the false gods that you see in today's culture.*

2. *How is our society being affected by removing God from our lives?*

3. *As a group, go to the back of the book to the Quick Reference Prayers and review the prayers so that in the week ahead you may use them as needed as you begin this study. These prayers are tested and full of God's promises. They are a good start to being effective in your prayer life.*

Week 1

OVERCOMING FEAR

I sought the LORD, and he answered me
and delivered me from all my fears.
Psalm 34:4 (ESV)

Lesson 1
WHERE DOES FEAR COME FROM?

Unbridled fear comes from the devil; it does not come from God. If you are afraid and have anxiety attacks during the day or in your dreams at night, they are not from God. He gives us power, love, and a sound mind. I have suffered from overwhelming fear for most of my adult life as well as gripping panic attacks. Only recently, God has shown me that I had to suffer, both physically and mentally, in order to learn how to fight the enemy. To experience victory I had to fully surrender to God and trust that my power comes from Jesus Christ, and then learn how to use the Word of God when the devil comes at me. Without a doubt, while you are on this earth, the devil will attack you or a loved one. God promised that once you learn to submit everything to Him and learn how to resist the devil, he will flee from you.

Heavenly Father, I pray that You will speak to me through Your Word and provide divine understanding of Your truth. Give me ears to hear and eyes to see and a heart to understand. In Jesus' name I pray, amen.

Be self-controlled and alert. Your enemy the devil prowls around like a roaring lion looking for someone to devour. *1 Peter 5:8*
For our struggle is not against flesh and blood, but against the rulers, against the authorities, against the powers of this dark world, and against the spiritual forces of evil in the heavenly realms. *Ephesians 6:12*

For God hath not given us the spirit of fear; but of power, and of love, and of a sound mind. 2 Timothy 1:7 (KJV)

So do not fear, for I am with you; do not be dismayed, for I am your God. I will strengthen you and help you; I will uphold you with my righteous right hand. Isaiah 41:10

There is no fear in love. But perfect love drives out fear, because fear has to do with punishment. The one who fears is not made perfect in love. 1 John 4:18

Submit yourselves, then, to God. Resist the devil and he will flee from you. James 4:7

God wants us to be courageous. We need to learn to use the authority we have been given by Jesus to resist the devil's attack. In Revelation 21:8 it is revealed that the cowardly are included in the second death and will be cast into the burning lake of sulfur…let's be courageous! I once read this quote on the billboard of a brake shop.

"COURAGE IS FEAR WITH PRAYER"

But Christ is faithful as a son over God's house. And we are his house, if we hold fast to our courage and the hope of which we boast. Hebrews 3:6

For you did not receive a spirit that makes you a slave again to fear, but you received the spirit of sonship. Romans 8:15

[As Jesus walked on water to the disciples in the boat he said to them] "Take courage! It is I. Don't be afraid." Then he climbed into the boat with them and the wind died down. Mark 6:50

Many ask the question, "Why does God allow the devil to exist?" The answer is that God gave us free will to *choose* our sinful nature (the flesh) that is influenced by the devil or to *choose* His way, which is guided by His Spirit, when we accept His Son. Lucifer was an angel with a privileged position who thought he knew better than God and could do it better than God. He chose to go against God and was thrown out of heaven. Adam and Eve also chose to go against God and listen to the serpent, and from this decision, sin entered the world.

Because we have free will and the devil is currently ruling on earth, we also need to *ask* for protection from the enemy. The devil will ultimately be destroyed by Jesus. Individually, we have to decide whether we will follow Jesus or not.

The God of peace will soon crush Satan under your feet. *Romans 16:20*

Journaling Exercise

1. List your fears.

2. Over time, what is God doing to remove them?

I had rather be a doorkeeper in the house of my God,
than to dwell in the tents of wickedness.
Psalm 84:10 (KJV)

Lesson 2
7 TOOLS TO RESIST THE DEVIL

1. Jesus' Name

Never forget the power of Jesus' name. God gave Him the name "Jesus" and placed it above all other names. At the name of Jesus, *every knee will* bow, in heaven and on earth, and under the earth.

Heavenly Father, I pray that You will speak to me through Your Word and provide divine understanding of Your truth. Give me ears to hear and eyes to see and a heart to understand. In Jesus' name I pray, amen.

Therefore God also has highly exalted Him and given Him the name which is above every name, that at the name of Jesus every knee should bow, of those in heaven, and of those on earth, and of those under the earth, and that every tongue should confess that Jesus Christ is Lord, to the glory of God the Father. *Philippians 2:9–11 (NKJV)*

Then Jesus came to them and said, "All authority in heaven and on earth has been given to me." *Matthew 28:18*

For I am persuaded, that neither death, nor life, nor angels, nor principalities, nor powers, nor things present, nor things to come, nor height, nor depth, nor any other creature, shall be able to separate us from the love of God which is in Christ Jesus our Lord. *Romans 8:38–39 (KJV)*

Before I was a Christian, I was physically attacked by the enemy. During the night, on about four occasions, he tightly gripped my juggler, and I couldn't utter a sound. He taunted me and told me what he would keep me from accomplishing. I would wake my husband, a Christian, to pray and eventually the fear would subside. Later on, after I accepted the Lord, he came again, but this time I forcefully spoke the words, "Jesus is Lord." He left immediately.

Jesus has absolute authority over Satan and all the principalities of darkness. Principalities are evil powers that oppose everything and everyone that is of God. This authority that Jesus has over Satan and his demons is ours to claim through His name and He has given us the authority to use His name. If you feel under physical or mental attack by Satan, and can only say, "Jesus Christ is Lord", he must flee. You can also say, "Jesus is my authority" or "In the name of Jesus, I command you to leave." Command evil to go away in the name of Jesus and claim that all your thoughts are held captive to the obedience of Jesus Christ. There can be a constant battle fighting fear and negativity at first, so use these words often. The enemy will come at you less and less as you grow in the strength of Jesus.

[Jesus said] "Truly, truly, I say to you, whoever believes in me will also do the works that I do; and greater works than these will he do, because I am going to the Father. Whatever you ask in my name, this I will do, that the Father may be glorified in the Son. If you ask me anything in my name, I will do it." John 14:12–14 (ESV)

The seventy-two returned with joy, saying "Lord, even the demons are subject to us in your name! And he said to them, "I saw Satan fall like lightning from heaven. Behold, I have given you authority to tread on serpents and scorpions, and over all the power of the enemy, and nothing shall hurt you." Luke 10:17–19 (ESV)

[Jesus said] "And these signs will follow those who believe: In my name they will cast out demons; they will speak with new tongues; they will take up serpents; and if they drink anything deadly, it will by no means hurt them; they will lay hands on the sick, and they will recover." Mark 16:17–18 (NKJV)

The weapons we fight with are not the weapons of the world. On the contrary, they have divine power to demolish strongholds. We demolish arguments and every pretension that sets itself up against the knowledge of God, and we take captive every thought to make it obedient to Christ. 2 Corinthians 10:4–5

Between dying on the cross and His resurrection on the third day, Jesus conquered death. Therefore, good has absolute power over evil. Jesus is victorious and the devil is defeated. Jesus holds the keys to death and Hades. This means that the devil cannot physically kill you and only Jesus has the authority to send someone to hell. As believers in Christ, death has lost its sting because we know the fiery outcome of the devil and our victory will be eternal life with Jesus.

[Jesus said] "Do not be afraid; I am the First and the Last. I am He who lives, and was dead, and behold, I am alive forevermore. Amen. And I have the keys of Hades and of Death." Revelation 1:17–18 (NKJV)

Since the children have flesh and blood, he too shared in their humanity so that by his death he might destroy him who holds the power of death—that is the devil—and free those who all their lives were held in slavery by their fear of death. Hebrews 2:14–15

But when this perishable will have put on the imperishable, and this mortal will have put on immortality, then will come about the saying that is written, "Death is swallowed up in victory. O death, where is your victory? O death, where is your sting?" The sting of death is sin, and the power of sin is the law; but thanks be to God, who gives us the victory through our Lord Jesus Christ. 1 Corinthians 15:54–57 (NASB)

2. Jesus' Blood

The blood Jesus shed for us on the cross is all powerful. We have been set free from our sins by His blood and it overcomes all the oppression of the enemy. His blood overpowers darkness and everything related to it. The book of Revelation reveals that the devil was overcome by the blood of the Lamb. From first-hand experience, I can tell you that when you feel under attack, you have only to say, "I plead the blood of Jesus over myself or another," and the devil must flee. Plead the blood of Jesus over your family, pets, home, and as you start your car for protection.

Heavenly Father, I pray that You will speak to me through Your Word and provide divine understanding of Your truth. Give me ears to hear and eyes to see and a heart to understand. In Jesus' name I pray, amen.

Who hath delivered us from the power of darkness, and hath translated us into the kingdom of his dear Son: In whom we have redemption through his blood, even the forgiveness of sins. Colossians 1:13–14 (KJV)

Not with the blood of goats and calves, but with His own blood He entered the Most Holy Place once for all, having obtained eternal redemption. For if the blood of bulls and goats and the ashes of a heifer, sprinkling the unclean, sanctifies for the purifying of the flesh, how much more shall the blood of Christ, who through the eternal Spirit offered Himself without spot to God, cleanse your conscience from dead works to serve the living God? Hebrews 9:12–14 (NKJV)

For you know that it was not with perishable things such as silver or gold that you were redeemed from the empty way of life handed down to you from your forefathers, but with the precious blood of Christ, a lamb without blemish or defect. 1 Peter 1:18–19

They overcame him [the devil] by the blood of the Lamb and by the word of their testimony, they did not love their lives so much as to shrink from death. Revelation 12:11

The precious blood of Jesus Christ was the price that was paid for the atonement of our sins. The balance is paid in full. We now have eternal life with God if we believe in His Son. Claim the power of the blood of Jesus by asking for it to be poured over you or a loved one for protection.

"Worthy are you to take the scroll and to open its seals, for you were slain, and by your blood you ransomed people for God from every

tribe and language and people and nation, and you have made them
a kingdom and priests to our God, and they shall reign on the earth."
Revelation: 5:9–10 (ESV)

3. Jesus' Light

Jesus is the light of the world. He came into the world to reveal His true light that gives light to us all. The definition of darkness is "the absence of light." Where Jesus' light is, there can be no darkness. Darkness does not like the light, so it cannot remain. New Age believers ask for "white light" but do not know the true source of the light, Jesus. When praying for protection, only ask for the light of Jesus to be present, because Satan masquerades as an angel of light.

> *And after six days Jesus took with him Peter and James, and John his*
> *brother, and led them up a high mountain by themselves. And he was*
> *transfigured before them, and his face shone like the sunshine, and his*
> *clothes became white as light.* Matthew 17:1–2
> *And no wonder for Satan himself masquerades as an angel of light.*
> 2 Corinthians 11:14

Before I became a Christian, I had a woman of great faith in Jesus come and bless my house. While there, she walked through and prayed for Jesus' light to fill our home so that I might find some much-needed peace. When I walked into our home after she left, the inside of the house literally shone with His light, especially in my bedroom. Evil cannot exist in the presence of Jesus' light. I'd had 10 miscarriages between this home and the little house next door. Shortly after her visit, I became pregnant and later gave birth to my daughter. During my pregnancy, there was a lot of prayer from my mother-in-law and her prayer group. Ask Jesus to fill your home with the light of His presence.

Heavenly Father, I pray that You will speak to me through Your Word and provide divine understanding of Your truth. Give me ears to hear and eyes to see and a heart to understand. In Jesus' name I pray, amen.

When Jesus spoke again to the people, he said, "I am the light of the world. Whoever follows me will never walk in darkness, but will have the light of life." John 8:12

All things were made through him, and without him was not anything made that was made. In him was life, and the life was the light of men. The light shines in the darkness, and the darkness has not overcome it. There was a man sent from God, whose name was John. He came as a witness, to bear witness about the light, that all might believe through him. He was not the light, but came to bear witness about the light. The true light, which gives light to everyone, was coming into the world. John 1:3–9 (ESV)

And this is the judgment: the light has come into the world, and people loved the darkness rather than the light because their works were evil. For everyone who does wicked things hates the light and does not come to the light, lest his works should be exposed. But whoever does what is true comes to the light, so that it may be clearly seen that his works have been carried out in God. John 3:19–21 (ESV)

This is the message we have heard from him and declare to you: God is light; in him there is no darkness at all. If we claim to have fellowship with him yet walk in the darkness, we lie and do not live by the truth. But if we walk in the light, as he is in the light, we have fellowship with one another, and the blood of Jesus, his Son purifies us from all sin. 1 John 1:5–7

The light of Jesus is the lamp on the stand that we must not hide. Ask for Jesus' light to shine through you to be a witness to others. His light in us attracts others to seek what we have.

[Jesus said] "You are the light of the world. A city set on a hill cannot be hidden. Nor do people light a lamp and put it under a basket, but on a stand, and it gives light to all in the house. In the same way, let your light shine before others, so that they may see your good works and give glory to your Father who is in heaven." Matthew 5:14–16 (ESV)

4. The Word

Resist the devil's lies with God's truth by reading and understanding your Bible. God's Word is living and active and sharper than any two-edged sword as we use it to fight the devil and his cohorts. The Bible reveals that all scripture is God-breathed by Him revealing His Word to the prophets and disciples that wrote them. Memorize scripture to receive the authority that God has placed in His Word.

During our earthly life, we must deal with the fact that the devil currently rules the earth and we are required to wage a spiritual battle against him. God is sovereign. He is the Ultimate Authority, so Satan is allowed to operate in the world within the boundaries that God sets for him. Satan does not have authority over the Word of God. After Jesus had been fasting for 40 days in the desert, the devil came to attack Him. Jesus rebuked the devil with the Word of God. Jesus said, "It is written"…and then quoted scripture. We must do the same.

Remember that Satan is a liar and the father of all lies. To resist these lies, we have to stand up to him in faithful obedience to biblical truth. God can never lie, and the truth of His Word is what sets us free. Do not allow deceiving spirits to alter what God's Word clearly shows us to be truth.

Heavenly Father, I pray that You will speak to me through Your word and provide divine understanding of Your truth. Give me ears to hear and eyes to see and a heart to understand. In Jesus' name I pray, amen.

For the word of God is living and powerful, and sharper than any two-edged sword, piercing even to the division of soul and spirit, and of joints and marrow, and is a discerner of the thoughts and intents of the heart. *Hebrews 4:12 (NKJV)*

All Scripture is God-breathed and is useful for teaching, rebuking, correcting and training in righteousness, so that the man of God may be thoroughly equipped for every good work. *2 Timothy 3:16–17*

You shall not add to the word that I command you, nor take from it, that you may keep the commandments of the Lord your God that I command you. *Deuteronomy 4:2 (ESV)*

"As for me, this is my covenant with them," says the LORD. "My Spirit, who is on you, and my words that I have put in your mouth will not depart from your mouth, or from the mouths of your children, or from the mouths of their descendants from this time on and forever," says the LORD." Isaiah 59:21

Jesus said to them, "If God were your Father, you would love me, for I came from God and now am here. I have not come on my own, but he sent me. Why is my language not clear to you? Because you are unable to hear what I say. You belong to your father, the devil, and you want to carry out your father's desire. He was a murderer from the beginning, not holding to the truth, for there is no truth in him. When he lies, he speaks his native language, for he is a liar and the father of lies." John 8:42–44

The coming of the lawless one is according to the working of Satan, with all power, signs, and lying wonders, and with all unrighteous deception among those who perish, because they did not receive the love of the truth, that they might be saved. 2 Thessalonians 2:9–10 (NKJV)

The Spirit clearly says that in later times some will abandon the faith and follow deceiving spirits and things taught by demons. Such teachings come through hypocritical liars, whose consciences have been seared as with a hot iron. 1 Timothy 4:1–2

Because God wanted to make the unchanging nature of his purpose very clear to the heirs of what was promised, he confirmed it with an oath. God did this so that, by two unchangeable things in which it is impossible for God to lie, we who have fled to take hold of the hope offered to us may be greatly encouraged. We have this hope as an anchor for the soul, firm and secure. Hebrews 6:17–19a

Another way to resist the devil's lies is to be very cognizant of what you listen to and what you watch. The Bible tells us that right now the devil is the "ruler of the kingdom of air" and he can use the airways as a foothold to enter our lives. This would include many aspects of television, movies, phone, internet, radio, online gaming, etc. I encourage you to ask God for discernment so that you are very selective about what your family is exposed to every day. Sometimes I find it necessary to plead the blood of Jesus over my computer and cell phone and all airways in between just for them to work correctly.

As for you, you were dead in your transgressions and sins, in which you used to live when you followed the ways of this world and of the ruler of the kingdom of the air, the spirit who is now at work in those who are disobedient. Ephesians 2:1–2

5. Praising God

Whenever you are under attack from the enemy, just start praising and thanking God and the devil must flee. Pray your thanks for His greatness, His love, His sovereignty, the overpowering glory that we see every day in His creation, and all His many blessings. God inhabits the praises of His people. He is right there when you are praising Him. Praise Him continually, for praise produces faith, and faith works love, and love never fails. The devil is defenseless against pure faith. In Luke 15:31, Satan wanted to go after Simon (Peter) but Jesus prayed that his faith would not fail. If ever you feel darkness come over you, praise God and feel His presence. Listening to Christian music on the radio allows us to sing and praise and be filled with His empowering Spirit.

Heavenly Father, I pray that You will speak to me through Your Word and provide divine understanding of Your truth. Give me ears to hear and eyes to see and a heart to understand. In Jesus' name I pray, amen.

Praise Him for His mighty deeds; praise Him according to His excellent greatness. Praise Him with trumpet sound; praise Him with harp and lyre. Praise Him with timbrel and dancing; praise Him with stringed instruments and pipe. Praise Him with loud cymbals; praise Him with resounding cymbals. Let everything that has breath praise the Lord. Praise the Lord! Psalm 150:2–6 (NASB)

But thou art holy. O thou that inhabitest the praises of Israel. Psalm 22:3 (KJV)

And they [the angels] do not rest day or night, saying: "Holy, holy, holy, is the Lord God Almighty, Who was, and is, and is to come!" Revelation 4:8b (NKJV)

Oh come, let us sing to the LORD! Let us shout joyfully to the Rock of our salvation. Let us come before His presence with thanksgiving; Let us shout joyfully to Him with psalms. Psalm 95:1–2 (NKJV)

Rejoice evermore. Pray without ceasing. In everything give thanks: for this is the will of God in Christ Jesus concerning you. 1 Thessalonians 5:16–18 (KJV)

6. His Church

The church is all of Jesus' people that together make up the Bride and Jesus is the Groom. Some glorious day we will meet together for the Wedding Supper of the Lamb. There will not be separate tables for every denomination. We need to unite as believers in Christ and hold fast to the truth revealed in God's Word of what brings salvation and what it means to be a follower of Christ.

Until that day, we are called to gather as believers to worship and learn more from God's Word and grow in our faith. It is important to go to a Bible-based church on a regular basis. On the Sabbath, Jesus attended the synagogue regularly because it was His custom. It is good to make it a family custom as well. The devil will give your family a lot of resistance to keep you from attending every week, but the more you faithfully attend, the less and less he will try.

As members of the body of Christ, we are given certain gifts (i.e. apostles, prophets, evangelists, pastors, teachers), that combine together to attain the unity of faith needed to succeed. Jesus is the head of the church and each member is a crucial body part that makes up the whole. We need to get in community with fellow Christians to walk this life and share in times of rejoicing, trials, and tribulations. God never intended for us to do this all alone. That is why He gave each of us certain gifts from the Spirit to combine with other's gifts. We must have an established circle of Christian friends that are there to lend support, lift one another up, pray earnestly for one other, and to lovingly hold each other accountable to biblical truth. In times of attack from the enemy or a seemingly unending supply of tribulation, we need the support and prayers of our Christian brothers and sisters.

Heavenly Father, I pray that You will speak to me through Your Word and provide divine understanding of Your truth. Give me ears to hear and eyes to see and a heart to understand. In Jesus' name I pray, amen.

He went to Nazareth, where he had been brought up and on the Sabbath day he went into the synagogue, as was his custom. *Luke 4:16*

And He Himself gave some to be apostles, some prophets, some evangelists, and some pastors and teachers, for the equipping of the saints for the work of ministry, for the edifying of the body of Christ, till we all come to the unity of the faith and of the knowledge of the Son of God, to a perfect man, to the measure of the stature of the fullness of Christ; that we should no longer be children, tossed to and fro and carried about with every wind of doctrine, by the trickery of men, in the cunning craftiness of deceitful plotting, but, speaking the truth in love, may grow up in all things into Him who is the head—Christ—from whom the whole body, joined and knit together by what every joint supplies, according to the effective working by which every part does its share, causes growth of the body for the edifying of itself in love. *Ephesians 4:11–16 (NKJV)*

We have different gifts, according to the grace given us. If a man's gift is prophesying, let him use it in proportion to his faith. If it is serving, let him serve; if it is teaching, let him teach; if it is encouraging, let him encourage, if it is contributing to the needs of others, let him give generously; if it is leadership, let him govern diligently, if it is showing mercy, let him do it cheerfully. *Roman 12:6–8*

And let us consider one another in order to stir up love and good works, not forsaking the assembling of ourselves together, as is the manner of some, but exhorting one another, and so much the more as you see the Day approaching. *Hebrews 10:24–25 (NKJV)*

Therefore confess your sins to each other and pray for each other so that you may be healed. The prayer of a righteous man is powerful and effective. *James 5:16*

> *As iron sharpens iron, so one man sharpens another.* Proverbs 27:17
>
> *[Jesus said] "Again I say to you, that if two of you agree on earth about anything that they may ask, it shall be done for them by My Father who is in heaven. For where two or three have gathered together in My Name, there I am in their midst."* Matthew 18:19 (NASB)
>
> *Two are better than one, because they have a good return for their work: if one falls down, his friend can help him up. But pity the man who falls and has no one to help him up!* Ecclesiastes 4:9–10

7. Jesus' Army

When Archangel Michael and his angels fought Lucifer in heaven, the devil, or dragon, was hurled down and took one-third of the angels with him. Two-thirds of the angels are still under the Army of Jesus and can be called on to minister, fight, and protect. Ask Jesus to call on them according to your needs. On road trips plead the blood of Jesus over your car and ask Jesus to send down guardian angels to surround and protect your vehicle. Ask Jesus for His ministering angels for those who you are praying for salvation. I pray for Jesus to send down ministering and warring (fighting, protecting, guarding, whichever you prefer) angels to keep my daughter safe and able to learn at school.

We know from the Bible of Archangel Michael who fights and Messenger Gabriel who guides and instructs. The rest of the angels we do not know by name. Here is a list of a variety of tasks carried out by these angels: (Reference: Dr. John Bechtle, Christiananswers.net)

- Worship and Praise: They do this in Heaven
- Messenger: Communicate God's will to man
- Guiding: Give instructions
- Providing: Provide physical needs (like Hagar when she was cast out)
- Protecting: Keep God's people out of physical danger
- Delivering: Get God's people out of danger
- Strengthening and encouraging: They strengthened Jesus while in the wilderness and encouraged Paul that everyone would survive the shipwreck
- Caring: Ministering to believers at the moment of death

Heavenly Father, I pray that You will speak to me through Your Word and provide divine understanding of Your truth. Give me ears to hear and eyes to see and a heart to understand. In Jesus' name I pray, amen.

Then another sign appeared in heaven: an enormous red dragon with seven heads and ten horns and seven crowns on his heads. His tail swept a third of the stars out of the sky and flung them to the earth. *Revelation: 12:3–4a*

Now war arose in heaven, Michael and his angels fighting against the dragon. And the dragon and his angels fought back, but he was defeated, and there was no longer any place for them in heaven. And the great dragon was thrown down, that ancient serpent, who is called the devil and Satan, the deceiver of the whole world—he was thrown down to the earth, and his angels were thrown down with him. *Revelation 12:7–9 (ESV)*

For he will command his angels concerning you to guard you in all your ways. On their hands they will bear you up, lest you strike your foot against a stone. *Psalm 91:11–12 (ESV)*

Are not all angels ministering spirits sent to serve those who will inherit salvation? *Hebrews 1:14*

[Temptation of Jesus] The Spirit immediately drove him out into the wilderness. And he was in the wilderness forty days, being tempted by Satan. And he was with the wild animals, and the angels were ministering to him. *Mark 1:12 (ESV)*

[Jesus said] "See that you do not look down on one of these little ones. For I tell you that their angels in heaven always see the face of my Father in heaven." *Matthew 18:10*

Jesus is above all the angels, they worship Him. When calling on angels for help, we must ask for Jesus to send them down. We want to make very certain we are not worshipping angels or calling the fallen angels of Satan. Remember that Satan is a liar and can twist things if we are not specific. Do not fall for the New Age beliefs of worshipping angels and calling them names that are not in the Bible. If you do, you are asking for trouble.

[John fell to his feet to worship the angel and the angel said] "Do not do it! I am a fellow servant with you and with your brothers who hold to the testimony of Jesus. Worship God! For the testimony of Jesus is the spirit of prophesy." Revelation 19:10

He is the radiance of the glory of God and the exact imprint of his nature, and he upholds the universe by the word of his power. After making purification for sins, he sat down at the right hand of the Majesty on high, having become as much superior to angels as the name he has inherited is more excellent than theirs. For to which of the angels did God ever say, "You are my Son, today I have begotten you."? Or again, "I will be to him a father, and he shall be to me a son."? And again, when he brings the firstborn into the world, he says, "Let all God's angels worship him." Hebrews 1:3–6 (ESV)

A Prayer to Combat the Enemy

Heavenly Father, I praise Your Holy Name. Thank you for sending down Your precious Son to shine His light and show us the truth of Your Word. **I claim the power of the light of Jesus to be present throughout this house** *[wherever you are]. Where there is Your light, there can be no darkness.*

Jesus, your perfect love casts out all fear. Fear has to do with punishment and You have taken ALL the punishment that I deserve. You said, "It is finished." I praise and thank you for Your perfect love on the cross! God placed You in the highest place and gave You the name that is above all names, and at the name of Jesus, all knees should bow, in heaven and on earth and under the earth, and every tongue confess that Jesus is Lord.

God did not give me a spirit of fear but of power, love, and a sound mind. I claim Your power and Your love over my mind and I call all my thoughts captive to the obedience of Jesus Christ.

Your Word is sharper than a two-edged sword, able to separate the joints from the marrow, and I claim Your words that "no weapon formed against me shall prosper." We were purchased for God at a price, by the precious blood of Jesus Christ. **I claim the power of the blood of Jesus over me** *and ask for You, Jesus, to send down warring angels to surround me and keep me safe. In Jesus' Mighty Name I pray, amen.*

Journaling Exercise

List the 7 tools you have been given to resist the devil.

He shall cover you with His feathers, And under His wings you shall take refuge; His truth shall be your shield and buckler.
Psalm 91:4 (NKJV)

Lesson 3
SLEEP IN PEACE

*P*rotection as you sleep is crucial. Each night before going to bed, pray for protection for yourself, your children, and other loved ones. Before our family started praying this prayer, our children were very afraid to sleep by themselves. We did <u>not</u> have peaceful dreams. Instead we slept fitfully, had nightmares, and were scared. The peace of the Lord is now tangibly felt in our house with this prayer. Our dreams are from Jesus and the Holy Spirit speaks verses and even worship songs as I sleep. Our children are well rested and do not wake up during the night. That's a praise!

Sleep is a precious commodity and a requirement for our bodies to regenerate and stay healthy. There are two other areas besides prayer that we can work on to attain better sleep. First, we are instructed in Ephesians 4:27, "Do not let the sun go down while you are still angry, and do not give the devil a foothold." Resolve all fights before you go to bed so the devil does not have an entrance into your sleep. Second, recall that in chapter two of Ephesians we learned that the devil is the prince, or owner, of the airways. Do not watch bad things on television or violent video games that give an opening for bad dreams from the enemy. Unplug before you go to bed. Turn off the Wi-Fi at the router box, or better yet, have it hardwired and do not keep your cell phone next to your bed. If you must have your phone, then place it on 'Airplane Mode' through the night. You can also purchase an alarm clock to plug in and have a home phone line. Your sleep will be so much more restful without the bombardment of internet interference and your home will be filled with the peace of the Lord after you pray the prayer below.

Heavenly Father, I pray that You will speak to me through Your Word and provide divine understanding of Your truth. Give me ears to hear and eyes to see and a heart to understand. In Jesus' name I pray, amen.

I will lie down and sleep in peace, for you alone, O LORD, make me dwell in safety. *Psalm 4:8*

My son, let them not vanish from your sight; keep sound wisdom and discretion, So they will be life to your soul and adornment to your neck. Then you will walk in your way securely and your foot will not stumble. When you lie down, you will not be afraid; when you lie down, your sleep will be sweet. *Proverbs 3:21–24 (NASB)*

For He will command his angels concerning you to guard you in all your ways; they will lift you up in their hands, so that you will not strike your foot against a stone. *Psalm 91:11–12*

And the peace of God, which surpasses all understanding, will guard your hearts and your minds in Christ Jesus. *Philippians 4:7(ESV)*

He will cover you with his feathers and under his wings you will find refuge; his faithfulness will be your shield and rampart. *Psalm 91:4*

A Nightly Prayer to Sleep in Peace

Heavenly Father, we thank you for all the blessings in our lives. (Tell Him what you are thankful for. Pray for those who need prayer.)

Lord Jesus, please fill this home with the light of Your presence. You are the Light of the World and where Your light is, there can be no darkness. I plead the blood of Jesus over this home as an umbrella of protection. I call on You, Jesus, to send down warring angels to guard and protect our doors so that no evil may enter and only good dwells within this home. I claim this house as a house of the LORD.

Jesus, please heal us with Your touch and restore our bodies as we sleep and keep us free from pain. Father, please place us under Your wing and give us dreams only from Jesus and words from the Holy Spirit. I pray that the peace of the LORD be upon each one of us and guard our hearts and minds in Christ Jesus throughout the night. You will keep in perfect peace him whose mind is steadfast, because he trusts in You. We trust You, LORD. In Jesus' precious name we pray, amen.

Journaling Exercise
1. Read Psalm 91.
2. List what protection you have as you sleep.

3. Try unplugging from Wi-Fi and your cell phone and recite this prayer every night for a week and record the results each night.

My shield is God Most High, who saves the upright in heart.
Psalm 7:10

Lesson 4
THE ARMOR OF GOD

We are fighting a spiritual battle with the enemy in our quest for God's perfect love. In the book of Revelation, the devil revealed that he is at war with anyone following God's commandments and anyone believing in Jesus Christ. There is a bull's eye on each of our chests and we need protection to resist these fiery darts.

We must put on the armor of God to be able to stand our ground against the evil principalities that try to harm us. Boldly, declaring it out loud, put this armor on yourself, your spouse, your children, and anyone else that needs protection each day. Whatever your morning routine is, make it a habit to claim the armor the first thing you do. It is better to do it before your children wake up to avoid any strife brought on from the enemy. I visually concentrate on each piece of the armor being placed on them. The devil tries to distract you when praying for others, so like the instructions for putting on your oxygen mask first when travelling on a plane with a child, put the armor of God on yourself first, and then it is much easier to pray it on your loved ones. Each day starts anew and there is power in the spoken word, so be diligent to put this armor on daily out loud. As you move closer and closer to Jesus, evil will try to win you back or attack a loved one, so put on His armor and stand firm!

Heavenly Father, I pray that You will speak to me through Your Word and provide divine understanding of Your truth. Give me ears to hear and eyes to see and a heart to understand. In Jesus' name I pray, amen.

Put on the full armor of God so you are able to stand up against the schemes of the devil; because our struggle is not against flesh and blood, but against the rulers, against the authorities, against the world powers of this darkness, and against the spiritual forces of evil in the heavenly realms. Ephesians 6:11–12*

Then the dragon was enraged at the woman and went off to make war against the rest of her offspring-those who obey God's commandments and hold to the testimony of Jesus. Revelation 12:17*

And also for me, that words may be given to me in <u>opening my mouth boldly</u> to proclaim the mystery of the gospel, for which I am an ambassador in chains that <u>I may declare it boldly as I ought to speak</u>. Ephesians 6:19–20 (ESV)*

Each day in the morning and out loud, it can be prayed like this:

Armor of God

Heavenly Father, I pray the armor of God on so that I may stand firm. I pray the Helmet of Salvation and the Breastplate of Righteousness secure on my chest. Gird my loins with the Truth and shod my feet with the Preparation of the Gospel of Peace. In one hand I wield the Shield of Faith to resist all fiery darts of the enemy, and the other the Sword of the Spirit which is the Word of God, sharper than any two-edged sword. In Jesus' name I pray the armor of God on and plead the blood of Jesus over me for protection. I loose anything not from Jesus and I bind all my thoughts captive to the obedience of Jesus Christ. God did not give me a spirit of fear, but power, love, and a sound mind. In Jesus' name I pray, amen.

Continue and substitute the name of a person and pray the armor of God on each of your loved ones.

There are seven weapons of the armor of God; the seventh being prayer. Pray for one another. The Bible tells us to pray without ceasing. We are the saints that Apostle Paul writes of in the following verses (Ephesians 6:18) when we believe in Jesus Christ and call on His name.

Therefore, take up the full armor of God, so that you may be able to resist in the evil day, and having done everything, to stand firm. Stand firm therefore, having girded your loins with truth, and having put on the breastplate of righteousness, and having shod your feet with the preparation of the gospel of peace; in addition to all, taking up the shield of faith with which you will be able to extinguish all the flaming arrows of the evil one. And take the helmet of salvation, and the sword of the Spirit, which is the word of God. With all prayer and petition pray at all times in the Spirit, and with this in view, be on the alert with all perseverance and petition for all the saints, Ephesians 6:13–18 (NASB)

I delight greatly in the LORD; my soul rejoices in my God. For he has clothed me with garments of salvation and arrayed me in a robe of righteousness, as a bridegroom adorns his head like a priest, and as a bride adorns herself with her jewels. Isaiah 61:10

To the church of God which is at Corinth, to those who have been sanctified in Christ Jesus, saints by calling, with all who in every place call upon the name of our Lord Jesus Christ... 1 Corinthians 1:2 (NASB)

Journaling Exercise

Draw a body and label the 7 weapons of the armor of God and what it represents.

For the word of the LORD is right; and all His work is trustworthy.
Psalm 33:4 (KJV)

Lesson 5

It is Written...

When Jesus fought the devil in the desert, He claimed, "It is written....", and quoted scripture. The devil had to flee. We are given the authority to break the strongholds that bind us and declare the power given to us through Jesus Christ and the love that God has for us. Here are some verses to memorize to rebuke physical attacks of the devil or fear and strongholds he tries to use against us. They are also to affirm your faith in Christ Jesus.

Heavenly Father, I pray that You will speak to me through Your Word and provide divine understanding of Your truth. Give me ears to hear and eyes to see and a heart to understand. In Jesus' name I pray, amen.

Begin each verse by saying **"It is written…"**

[Jesus said] "Away from me, Satan! For it is written: 'Worship the Lord your God, and serve him only.'" Matthew 4:10

If God is for us, who can be against us? Romans 8:31b

And the peace of God, which surpasses all understanding, will guard your hearts and your minds in Christ Jesus. Philippians 4:7(ESV)

That at the name of Jesus every knee should bow, of things in heaven, and things in earth, and things under the earth. Philippians 2:10 (KJV)

There is now no condemnation for those who are in Christ Jesus. Romans 8:1

We take captive every thought to make it obedient to Christ. 2 Corinthians 10:5b

They said, "Believe in the Lord Jesus, and you will be saved, you and your household." Acts 16:31 (NASB)

The LORD is my light and my Salvation—whom shall I fear? Psalm 27:1a

The LORD is my shepherd, I shall not want. Psalm 23:1 (NASB)

The LORD is for me; I will not fear; what can man do to me? Psalm 118:6 (NASB)

To Him who loved us and washed us from our sins in His own blood, and has made us kings and priests to His God and Father, to Him be glory and dominion forever and ever. Amen. Revelation 1:5b–6b (NKJV)

For God hath not given us the spirit of fear; but of power, and of love, and of a sound mind. 2 Timothy 1:7 (KJV)

There is no fear in love. But perfect love casts out fear. 1 John 4:18 (ESV)

No weapon formed against you shall prosper. Isaiah 54:17 (NKJV)

[Jesus said] "Get behind Me, Satan!" Matthew 16:23a (NKJV)

You are all sons of God through faith in Christ Jesus. Galatians 3:26

If you belong to Christ, then you are Abraham's seed, and heirs according to the promise. Galatians 3:29

I can do all things through Christ who strengthens me. Philippians 4:13 (NKJV)

But he was wounded for our transgressions; he was crushed for our iniquities; upon him was the chastisement that brought us peace, and with his stripes we are healed. Isaiah 53:5 (ESV)

Being confident of this, that he who began a good work in you will carry it on to completion until the day of Christ Jesus. Philippians 1:6

[Jesus said] "My grace is sufficient for you, for my power is made perfect in weakness." 2 Corinthians 12:9a

"For I know the plans I have for you," declares the Lord, "plans to prosper you and not to harm you, plans to give you hope and a future." Jeremiah 29:11

I meditate on your precepts and consider your ways. I delight in your decrees: I will not neglect your word. Psalm 119:15–16

Journaling Exercise
Please listen online to "Word of God Speak" by MercyMe.

1. Meditate on the above verses of "It is Written…" and close your eyes and commune with God.
2. Write your experience. Which of these verses really spoke to you?

WEEK 1
GROUP QUESTIONS

1. How has fear affected your life? Read Ephesians 6:12 and discuss where our battle on this earth comes from.

2. Review the 7 tools to resist the devil. What weapon have you used in the past that has worked? Does anyone have a story where an angel has protected you?

3. How has prayer affected your sleep? Does anyone have a story about turning the Wi-Fi and cell phone off at night?

4. Recite together the armor of God and try to commit it to memory.

5. In the lesson "It is written…" please share what verse really spoke to you.

6. End in prayer and ask if there are any fears that you need to give over to Jesus.

Week 2

SALVATION

By the word of the LORD the heavens were made, and by the breath of his mouth all their host. He gathers the waters of the sea as a heap; he puts the deeps in storehouses.
Psalm 33:6–7(ESV)

Lesson 6

ONE TRUE INTERCESSOR

*J*esus was there in the beginning with God as "the Word." He is now our high priest that sits at the right hand of God as our intercessor. As our intercessor, when we pray in His name, we are praying directly to God. He is the one and only Son of God and the Son of Man at the same time. When He walked this earth, those that saw Him, saw God. Jesus tells us that no one can get to the Father but through the Son and we can call on His power at anytime. He knows our plights because He lived and suffered as fully human while still being fully God in the flesh.

Heavenly Father, I pray that You will speak to me through Your Word and provide divine understanding of Your truth. Give me ears to hear and eyes to see and a heart to understand. In Jesus' name I pray, amen.

In the beginning was the Word, and the Word was with God, and the Word was God. He was with God in the beginning...The Word became flesh, and made his dwelling among us. We have seen his glory, the glory of the One and Only, who came from the Father, full of grace and truth. *John 1:1 & John 1:14*

[Jesus said] "I have brought you glory on earth by completing the work you gave me to do. And now, Father, glorify me in your presence with the glory I had with you before the world began." *John 17:4–5*

Who will bring any charge against those whom God has chosen? It is God who justifies. Who is he that condemns? Christ Jesus, who died— more than that, who was raised to life—is at the right hand of God and is also interceding for us. Romans 8:33–34

Jesus answered, "I am the way and the truth and the life. No one comes to the Father except through me. If you really knew me, you would know my Father as well. From now on, you do know him and have seen him." John 14:6–7

[Jesus said] "Whoever believes in him is not condemned, but whoever does not believe stands condemned already because he has not believed in the name of God's one and only Son." John 3:18

Jesus said to them, "If God were your Father, you would love me, for I came from God and now am here, I have not come on my own, but he sent me." John 8:42

Jesus heard that they had cast him out; and when He had found him, He said to him, "Do you believe in the Son of Man?" He answered and said, "Who is He, Lord, that I may believe in Him?" And Jesus said to him, "You have both seen Him and it is He who is talking with you." John 9:35–37 (NKJV)

[Jesus said] "All things have been committed to me by my Father. No one knows the Son except the Father, and no one knows the Father except the Son and those to whom the Son chooses to reveal him. Come to me, all you who are weary and burdened, and I will give you rest. Take my yoke upon you and learn from me, for I am gentle and humble in heart, and you will find rest for your souls. For my yoke is easy and my burden is light." Matthew 11:27–30

Therefore, since we have a great high priest who has passed through the heavens, Jesus the Son of God, let us hold fast our confession. For we do not have a high priest who cannot sympathize with our weaknesses, but One who has been tempted in all things as we are, yet without sin. Therefore let us draw near with confidence to the throne of grace, so that we may receive mercy and find grace to help in time of need. Hebrews 4:14–16 (NASB)

Because Jesus died in His earthly body and ascended, the Holy Spirit or "Counselor" or "Comforter" can now reside in us and give us wisdom and revelation. The Spirit can also intercede on our behalf with God even when we don't know how to pray. Greater is the Spirit within you than any force on this earth, which includes the devil. The Holy Spirit was also there in the beginning as the "Spirit of God" hovering over the waters. This is the tri-head that explains that the Father, Son, and Holy Spirit are one God in three manifestations. All three work together to redeem our souls for eternity.

[Jesus said] "If you love me, you will obey what I command. And I will ask the Father and he will give you another Counselor to be with you forever—the Spirit of truth. The world cannot accept him, because it neither sees him nor knows him. But you know him, for he lives with you and will be in you. I will not leave you as orphans; I will come to you. Before long the world will not see me anymore, but you will see me. Because I live, you also will live. On that day you will realize that I am in my Father, and you are in me, and I am in you." John 14:15–20

You, dear children, are from God and have overcome them, because the one who is in you is greater than the one who is in the world. 1 John 4:4

In the same way, the Spirit helps in our weakness. We do not know what we ought to pray for, but the Spirit himself intercedes for us with groans that words cannot express. And he who searches our hearts knows the mind of the Spirit, because the Spirit intercedes for the saints in accordance with God's will. Romans 8:26–27

In the beginning God created the heavens and the earth. Now the earth was formless and empty, darkness was over the surface of the deep, and the Spirit of God was hovering over the waters. Genesis 1:1–2

Know in your heart that Jesus is God—past, present, and future.

"Behold, I am coming quickly, and My reward is with Me, to render to every man according to what he has done. I am the Alpha and the

Omega, the first and the last, the beginning and the end." Revelation
22:12–13 (NASB)

Journaling Exercise

1. Please listen online to the song "What Do I Know of Holy" by Addison
Road.

2. Draw a picture of a winter scene: First draw a lake. Next, draw a shore with
a tree at the bank with freshly laden snow. Last, draw clouds in the sky.

3. What do each of these have in common? They are all made from water but
are in different forms. This is an analogy of how God is God, but can be in
three forms to make up the Father, Son, and Holy Spirit.

Even the sparrow has found a home, and the swallow a nest for herself,
where she may have her young—a place near your altar
Psalm 84:3

Lesson 7
DIE TO SIN

*J*esus endured so much pain so that our sins would not be counted against us. He was whipped and scourged, stripped naked, made to wear a scarlet robe and a piercing crown of thorns, mocked, spat on and beaten over the head again and again, shouted at with many insults, burdened by the weight of the cross that He carried on His back, and finally nailed to the cross to die a torturous, hard to take a breath, death. We are no longer bound to the sin of Adam. Jesus took on himself all our sins, shame, and humiliation and overcame them. It is finished and our debt is paid in full.

Heavenly Father, I pray that You speak to me through Your Word and provide divine understanding of Your truth. Give me ears to hear and eyes to see and a heart to understand. In Jesus' name I pray, amen.

But he was pierced for our transgressions, he was crushed for our iniquities; the punishment that brought us peace was upon him, and by his wounds we are healed. We all, like sheep, have gone astray, each of us has turned to his own way; and the LORD has laid on him the iniquity of us all. *Isaiah 53:5–6*

He himself bore our sins in his body on the tree, so that we might die to sins and live for righteousness; by his wounds you have been healed. *1 Peter 2:24*

Then he released Barabbas to them; and when he had scourged Jesus, he delivered Him to be crucified. Then the soldiers of the governor took Jesus into the Praetorium and gathered the whole garrison around Him. And they stripped Him and put a scarlet robe on Him. When they had twisted a crown of thorns, they put it on His head, and a reed in His right hand. And they bowed the knee before Him and mocked Him, saying, "Hail, King of the Jews!" Then they spat on Him, and took the reed and struck Him on the head. And when they had mocked Him, they took the robe off Him, put His own clothes on Him, and led Him away to be crucified. Matthew 27:26–31 (NKJV)*
When Jesus had received the sour wine, he said, "It is finished," and he bowed his head and gave up his spirit.* John 19:30 (ESV)

The one man that brought us condemnation and death through his sin was Adam, and the one man who brought us righteousness and eternal life is Jesus.

> *For if, by the trespass of the one man, death reigned through that one man, how much more will those who receive God's abundant provision of grace and of the gift of righteousness reign in life through the one man, Jesus Christ. Consequently, just as the result of one trespass was condemnation for all men, so also the result of one act of righteousness was justification that brings life for all men.* Romans 5:17–18

The Bible instructs us that the house of David and the inhabitants of Jerusalem will recognize Jesus after the nations of the earth come against her. They will mourn and grieve the death of Jesus as a parent mourns the death of their child. Some of you have experienced the depths of this grief of losing a child personally. Others of us can only try to fathom the depths of this pain as we mourn that Jesus hung on the cross not because of his faults, but for our sins. Please don't miss the significance of what Jesus did for you.

> *And I will pour out on the house of David and the inhabitants of Jerusalem a spirit of grace and supplication. They will look on me, the one they have pierced, and they will mourn for him as one mourns for*

an only child, and grieve bitterly for him as one grieves for a first-born son. Zechariah 12:10

A Prayer of Thanks

Lord Jesus, in the Garden of Gethsemane Your sweat was like drops of blood when thinking of the torture that was to come the next day. Even Your closest friends abandoned You in Your hour of need. You acted in complete obedience as You turned Yourself over to the authorities and accepted the verdict of death on the cross. You selflessly took on all the punishment, humiliation, and shame that we deserved so that they might be removed from us. Your body was broken for us to be healed and Your blood poured out so that our sins would be forgiven. Oh how can it be, that my King would die for me? Thank you, Lord Jesus, for this ultimate act of love for us. I praise Your Great Name.

Journaling Exercise

1. Are you bound to the sinful nature of Adam or the abundance of grace that comes from the gift of righteousness in Christ?

2. Please listen online to the song "My Sweet Lord" by Crowder and Emmylou Harris (Neon Steeple album version). It is always easier to find music on the web when you type "song" and then the title.
3. Write your thoughts about this lovely song.

They that sow in tears shall reap in joy.
Psalm 126:5 (KJV)

Lesson 8

SHAME AND GUILT

*W*hen you burn with shame every time you think of sins you have committed or were committed against you, the devil is trying to condemn. You must not give him a weapon to form against you. Shame was introduced in the Garden of Eden when Adam and Eve realized they were naked after they disobeyed God. Jesus carried your shame and guilt when he died on the cross.

When you accept Jesus as your Lord, God keeps His promise that our sins will be remembered no more. You are forgiven by your Father and redeemed by the blood of the Lamb. Jesus took all those whippings across His back, all the mocking, so that all of us would stop beating ourselves up over shame and guilt. When our sins are uncovered and out of the dark, the light of Jesus sets us free, we are separated from them forever. His last uttered words were, "It is finished."

To release the burden of this shame and guilt, you might need to ask for forgiveness from the person you wronged. I have done this and believe me it was a burden removed off my shoulders. When you do ask for forgiveness, humbly ask this person to forgive you, give the matter all over to Jesus, and be released of its power over you. You can ask that Jesus place His yoke upon you, for His load is light and His burdens are few. Once you have repented from this shame or guilt, do not let condemnation come over you. Rebuke these thoughts and claim that you have been delivered from this action and Jesus suffered this shame for you at the cross.

Heavenly Father, I pray that You will speak to me through Your Word and provide divine understanding of Your truth. Give me ears to hear and eyes to see and a heart to understand. In Jesus' name I pray, amen.

...the eyes of both of them were opened, and they knew that they were naked; and they sewed fig leaves together and made themselves coverings. *Genesis 3:7 (NKJV)*

[Jesus said] "For God did not send His Son into the world to condemn the world, but that the world through Him might be saved. He who believes in Him is not condemned." *John 3:17–18a (NKJV)*

Stand fast therefore in the liberty by which Christ has made us free, and do not be entangled again with a yoke of bondage. *Galatians 5:1 (NKJV)*

[Jesus said] "Neither do I condemn you; go and sin no more." *John 8:11b (NKJV)*

And Jesus answered and said to them, "It is not those who are well who need a physician, but those who are sick. I have not come to call the righteous but sinners to repentance." *Luke 5:31–32 (NASB)*

And He said to me, "My grace is sufficient for you, for My strength is made perfect in weakness." *2 Corinthians 12:9 (NKJV)*

Journaling Exercise

1. List with a single word what has shamed you and what you feel guilty about. Lay your shame and guilt at the foot of the cross. If you can, call up or email the person you have wronged and ask for forgiveness.

2. Please listen online to the song, "What Love Really Means" by J.J. Heller and write down your thoughts and reflections.

Create in me a pure heart, O God, And renew a steadfast spirit within me.
Psalm 51:10 (NASB)

Lesson 9

GOD'S GRACE ABOUNDS

God gave us *GRACE*: *G*od's *R*iches *A*t *C*hrist's *E*xpense

S alvation is possible because Christ died on the cross. He was the ultimate and final sacrificial lamb needed for us to be forgiven. God is holy and just. Because He loved us so, He had to sacrifice His perfect Son for us to be reconciled with Him. All of our sins and the punishment that we deserved were put upon Jesus as He knowingly accepted the will of Father God to be crucified. His ultimate sacrifice made it possible for us to be forgiven and His righteousness transfers to us when we have faith in Jesus Christ. This is called transference. Though we are all messed-up sinners, God's grace abounds even greater. Now, Jesus is at the right hand of God and full of righteousness, and so are we in this world when we put our faith in Him.

Heavenly Father, I pray that You will speak to me through Your Word and provide divine understanding of Your truth. Give me ears to hear and eyes to see and a heart to understand. In Jesus' name I pray, amen.

> **And God raised us up with Christ and seated us with him in the heavenly realms in Christ Jesus, in order that in the coming ages he might show the incomparable riches of his grace, expressed in his kindness to us in Christ Jesus. For it is by grace you have been saved, through faith—and**

this not from yourselves, it is the gift of God—not by works, so no one can boast. Ephesians 2:6–9

For you know the grace of our Lord Jesus Christ, that though he was rich, yet for your sakes he became poor, so that you, through his poverty might become rich. 2 Corinthians 8:9

For while we were still helpless, at the right time Christ died for the ungodly. For one will hardly die for a righteous man; though perhaps for the good man someone would dare even to die. But God demonstrates His own love toward us, in that while we were yet sinners, Christ died for us. Romans 5:6–8 (NASB)

Once you were alienated from God and were enemies in your minds because of your evil behavior. But now he has reconciled you by Christ's physical body through death to present you holy in his sight, without blemish and free from accusation—if you continue in your faith, established and firm, not moved from the hope held out in the gospel. Colossians 1:21–23a

We implore you on behalf of Christ, be reconciled to God. For our sake he made him to be sin who knew no sin, so that in him we might become the righteousness of God. 2 Corinthians 5:20–21 (ESV)

This righteousness from God comes through faith in Jesus Christ to all who believe. There is no difference, for all have sinned and fall short of the glory of God, and are justified freely by his grace through the redemption that came by Jesus Christ. Romans 3:22–24

Moreover the law entered, that the offense might abound. But where sin abounded, grace did much more abound. Romans 5:20 (NKJV)

Journaling Exercise

1. Look up online Isaiah Chapter 53 (New King James Version) to read the prophesy of Jesus, the Man of Sorrows. Jot down the lines that really stand out to you.

2. Please listen online to the song "Call it Grace" by Unspoken and "Man of Sorrows" by Hillsong Live. After you have listened to these songs, if you feel the prompting of the Holy Spirit to accept Jesus as Lord of your life, go on to Lesson 10.

Wash me thoroughly from my iniquity, and cleanse me from my sin.
Psalm 51:2 (NKJV)

Lesson 10
THE SINNER'S PRAYER

*I*f you have never received Jesus into your life, or need to ask Him back into your life, pray out loud for Jesus' grace with the prayer below. Confess that you are a sinner in need of a Savior. You have been spiritually blind, and you want to see. Invite Jesus to be Lord of your life and confess this to someone else as a witness. You will then be reconciled with God, justified in His eyes, and have salvation. Remember, Jesus did not come to call the righteous, but for the sinner to be reconciled.

Heavenly Father, I pray that You will speak to me through Your Word and provide divine understanding of Your truth. Give me ears to hear and eyes to see and a heart to understand. In Jesus' name I pray, amen.

If we claim to be without sin, we deceive ourselves and the truth is not in us. If we confess our sins, he is faithful and just and will forgive us our sins and purify us from all unrighteousness. *1 John 1:8–9*

"The word is near you; it is in your mouth and in your heart," that is the word of faith proclaiming: That if you confess with your mouth, "Jesus is Lord", and believe in your heart that God raised him from the dead, you will be saved. *Romans 10:8–9*

[Jesus said] "I am the resurrection and the life. He who believes in me will live, even though he dies, and whoever lives and believes in me will never die." *John 11:25–26a*

Jesus answered them, "It is not the healthy who need a doctor, but the sick. I have not come to call the righteous, but sinners to repentance." Luke 5:32

[Paul wrote to Timothy] Christ Jesus came into the world to save sinners-of whom I am the worst. But for that very reason I was shown mercy so that in me, the worst of sinners, Christ Jesus might display his unlimited patience as an example for those who would believe on him and receive eternal life. 1 Timothy 1:15–16

Two criminals hung beside Jesus at Calvary. One yelled accusations at Jesus and told Him that if He was really who He said He was, to get them out of this mess. The other criminal realized who Jesus really was, God in flesh. This thief was saved by Jesus right then and there because he understood that he was a sinner, Jesus did not deserve to die, and that Jesus is Lord. Everything that you have listed as fears, shame, guilt, and sins can be given to Jesus. Lay these burdens at the foot of the cross where Jesus' blood was poured out on them. Jesus died for the glory of God and for you.

One of the criminals who were hanged there was hurling abuse at Him, saying, "Are You not the Christ? Save Yourself and us!" But the other answered, and rebuking him said, "Do you not even fear God, since you are under the same sentence of condemnation? And we indeed are suffering justly, for we are receiving what we deserve for our deeds; but this man has done nothing wrong." And he was saying, "Jesus, remember me when You come in Your kingdom!" And He said to him, "Truly I say to you, today you shall be with Me in Paradise." Luke 23:39–43 (NASB)

A Sinner's Prayer: *to be prayed out loud*
(Adapted from: "The Sinner's Prayer" www.intothelight.org)
"Heavenly Father, have mercy on me, a wretched sinner. I believe in You and that Your Word is true. I believe that Jesus Christ is the Son of the living God and that He died on the cross so that I may now have forgiveness for my sins and have eternal life with You.

I believe that You, LORD God, raised Him from the dead. Please, Lord Jesus, forgive me, for every sin I have ever committed and by Your blood cleanse me of all unrighteousness. I invite You into my heart as my personal Lord and Savior today. I have been spiritually blind, and I want to see. I need Your eternal friendship and love in my life. I give You my life and ask You to take full control from this moment on. I pray this in the name of Jesus Christ." Amen.

Speak to a pastor or another believer if you just confessed this alone and remember the parable of the farmer who planted the seed on good soil and by persevering produced a good crop. God chose you to be saved through the sanctifying work of the Spirit and through your belief in the truth. To be sanctified means, according to Webster's dictionary, the state of growing in divine grace as a result of Christian commitment after baptism or conversion (accepting Christ as your Lord and Savior) and also means to set us apart for holy use. You are now on the path to growing in the image of Jesus Christ because Jesus has imparted, or transferred, His holiness to you when you believe in Him. Christ is within you.

> ***But we ought always to thank God for you, brothers loved by the Lord, because from the beginning God chose you to be saved through the sanctifying work of the Spirit and through belief in the truth.***
> *2 Thessalonians 2:13*

You have been set free and are now in Christ! You have hope for your future because you will see Jesus in Heaven! You will no longer be afraid to die. Jesus is rejoicing! Angels in Heaven are rejoicing! Your name is written in the Book of Life and the enemy cannot take this from you. He has no claim to your salvation: walk in the light and stay in the truth.

> ***[Jesus said] "Likewise, I say to you, there is joy in the presence of the angels of God over one sinner who repents."*** *Luke 15:10 (NKJV)*
> ***[Jesus said] "However, do not rejoice that the spirits submit to you, but rejoice that your names are written in heaven."*** *Luke 10:20*

And all that dwell upon the earth shall worship him, whose names are not written in the book of life of the Lamb slain from the foundation of the world. Revelation 13:8 (KJV)

The minute you accept Jesus as your Lord and Savior, the enemy will come against you in full force. He will try to tell you that you are not really saved, try to convince you those words meant nothing, and try to make you doubt the validity of what you have confessed. This is not true. Once you confess these words out loud, you are saved. There is nothing that the devil can do to take this away. You have been sanctified by the blood of Christ through your confession. If you feel panic or attack, you can recite out loud the putting on of the armor of God and plead the blood of Jesus to cover you.

Journaling Exercise
1. Please listen online to "At the Cross" (Passion 2014) by Chris Tomlin.
2. Journal your story, God's story for you, of when you were saved.

As I began putting this book together, I was reluctant to share my personal stories. I thought this book was about God, not me. Three people independently told me that my story is really God's story. We all have a unique story as He seeks us out. The book of Revelation tells us that the enemy was overcome by the blood of the Lamb and *the words of their testimony.* (Revelation 12:11) Our stories give validity and witness to the miracles of God and how He loves us so.

My Testimony

The first time I felt the presence of God was also one of my earliest memories as a child. I was almost four years old and playing outside in the backyard in the dirt, digging up rolly polly bugs with a spoon. I sensed the presence of something much bigger than me. I felt God's love on me like a beam of sunshine. I'll never forget feeling so loved. Growing up, though my parents were not believers, I would often ask to go to church with neighbors because it just felt like what I should be doing. I felt empty on Sunday if I wasn't attending church. I always believed in God, but also believed the lie that Jesus was just a man.

I did not accept Jesus as my Lord and Savior until I was an adult. When I did, the pastor asked those who wanted to accept the Lord to rise, and I actually felt a push up from my bottom that gave me little choice but to stand and declare my acceptance of Jesus and all He had done for me. In the beginning, every time I saw or heard about Jesus' suffering on the cross, I cried. It still chokes me up. When I was baptized I gave my testimony in front of hundreds and I was very nervous until I felt a light come upon me, which I knew was the Holy Spirit. I was calmed and gave a strengthened testimony of being so lost and completely broken when Jesus found me. I was blind, but now I see the grace of Jesus. I told of my sorrow caused by reoccurring miscarriages and also my first personal encounter with Jesus right before I had accepted Him as my Lord and Savior. Though I gave a short version to the congregation, below is a more detailed description of the period leading up to my acceptance of Jesus as my Savior.

I had been very sick for months and I was not able to eat without having severe spasm reactions in my esophagus. I was diagnosed with eosinophilic esophagitis and my other symptoms included a leaky gut that caused me to become allergic to over 50 foods, severe migraines, and rapid weight loss. A lot of this illness was brought on from family strife, an overdose of pesticide exposure at work, and the stress of always worrying about my daughter's asthma that would sometimes hospitalize her.

It was at this point that I decided to fly to my parents' house with my daughter in the hopes that we would both get better in a warmer climate. During a period of a month and a half, I lost 20 pounds, was rarely able to sleep, and struggled to find anything that I could eat. My throat felt restricted and the lymph nodes in my neck were clogged and bubbling. I ended up in the E.R. with a heartbeat of 280 and the doctor attempted three times to inject medicine to stop and then reset my heart. The last injection worked because I asked the doctor on call at the little hospital to hold my hand. I had known him from the past to be a calm and loving doctor. Basically, with everything going on, I was having a mental and physical breakdown.

Shortly after I was released from the hospital, I remember walking the aisles of a health food store frantically looking for anything that might fix me. I came out of the store and was barely able to walk as I went to the waiting truck of an old family friend. I told him that he needed to take me to a hospital that would give me drugs so that I would no longer feel anything. He told me that they don't let you out of there, and I told him I didn't care. He refused to take me and drove me to the beach instead. He watched my daughter as I climbed down to the narrow shore and just laid there with my face plastered to the wet sand. When I woke up, the tide was coming in and sand flies were jumping all over my face and for a brief second, I thought I was dead. That was my lowest point, rock bottom you would say, and I decided that day that it couldn't get any worse than this, and I was going to live.

When I came back home after that month and a half, my husband didn't recognize me in the airport and my son had to point me out because I had grown so thin. I continued to have symptoms and strong pains in my organs as my mother-in-law cared for me. She told me that God had revealed to her that I was in a battle for my life with the enemy. In desperation, I drove to a nearby empty church with a door that was thankfully unlocked. I entered and went to the altar and knelt down in front of two elevated statues of Jesus and Mary and bowed my head and clasped my hands. I half expected to hear from Mary because I did not know Jesus very well. I cried out and pleaded for help. So clearly, I audibly heard Jesus' voice tell me, "This too shall pass." That was the moment that I truly knew that Jesus existed.

Shortly after this experience was when I attended a church for the first time and the pastor asked those who wanted to accept the Lord to rise. Over the next years, I held tightly to Jesus' promise that my symptoms would pass as I studied His Word and wrote this book during my trials. My food allergies are gone and every once in a while I will get a migraine that reminds me that when I am weak, He is strong.

WEEK 2
GROUP QUESTIONS

1. Discuss what being an intercessor means to you.

2. Have someone explain the Holy Trinity. This concept is bigger than our mind can completely comprehend.

3. What is the gift of righteousness?

4. Explain the acronym of GRACE.

5. Did anyone in your group ask Jesus into their heart and say the Sinner's Prayer?

6. Share your story of how you were brought to the foot of the cross and accepted Jesus as your Lord and Savior. Your story is God's story of how He brought you back to Him.

7. Take prayer requests and pray for each other throughout the week ahead.

Week 3

FORGIVENESS

I will say to the LORD, "My refuge and my fortress, my God, in whom I trust."
Psalm 91:2 (ESV)

Lesson 11

FACING EVIL

To face a person that is acting with malice towards you is difficult and feels uncomfortable. The Bible instructs us to face evil with good, and contrary to our nature, to love and pray for our enemies. We must remember that we do not know the plan that God has for them. Jesus died on the cross to enable every single person to be saved. Pray for them to know His love. This does not mean you or your family should be placed in harm's way, but as best as we can, we must be at peace with all men. When dealing with someone who may be angry or distant in Romans 12:15, it says, "Rejoice with those who rejoice, and weep with those who weep." Sending a card or phoning them to share in a happy occasion, or even a sad one, helps heal personal relationships.

Heavenly Father, I pray that You will speak to me through Your Word and provide divine understanding of Your truth. Give me ears to hear and eyes to see and a heart to understand. In Jesus' name I pray, amen.

Never pay back evil for evil to anyone. Respect what is right in the sight of all men. If possible, so far as it depends on you, be at peace with all men. Never take your own revenge, beloved, but leave room for the wrath of God, for it is written, "Vengeance is Mine, I will repay," says the Lord. "But if your enemy is hungry, feed him, and if he is thirsty, give him a drink; for in so doing, you will heap burning coals

on his head." Do not be overcome by evil, but overcome evil with good. Romans 12:17–21(NASB)

Do not repay evil with evil or insult with insult, but with blessing, because to this you were called so that you may inherit a blessing. For, "Whoever would love life and see good days must keep his tongue from evil and his lips from deceitful speech. He must turn from evil and do good; he must seek peace and pursue it for the eyes of the Lord are on the righteous and his ears are attentive to their prayer, but the face of the Lord is against those who do evil." 1 Peter 3:9–12

[Jesus said] "You have heard that it was said, 'Love your neighbor and hate your enemy.' But I tell you; Love your enemies and pray for those who persecute you, that you may be sons of your Father in heaven." Matthew 5:43–45a

[Jesus said] If you love those who love you, what credit is that to you? For even sinners love those who love them. If you do good to those who do good to you, what credit is that to you? For even sinners do the same. If you lend to those from whom you expect to receive, what credit is that to you? Even sinners lend to sinners in order to receive back the same amount. But love your enemies, and do good, and lend, expecting nothing in return; and your reward will be great, and you will be sons of the Most High; for He Himself is kind to ungrateful and evil men. Be merciful, just as your Father is merciful. Luke 6:32–36 (NASB)

Jesus replied, "Love the Lord your God with all your heart and with all your soul and with all your mind. This is the first and greatest commandment. And the second is like it: Love your neighbor as yourself." Matthew 22:37–39

When we are clothed in the robe of Jesus' righteousness, our enemies become God's enemies.

The LORD says to my Lord: "Sit at my right hand until I make your enemies a footstool for your feet." Psalm 110:1

So truth fails, and he who departs from evil makes himself a prey. Then the LORD saw it, and it displeased Him that there was no justice. He saw that there was no man, and wondered that there was no intercessor; therefore His own arm brought salvation for Him; and His own righteousness, it sustained Him. For He put on righteousness as a breastplate, and a helmet of salvation on His head; He put on the garments of vengeance for clothing, and was clad with zeal as a cloak. According to their deeds, accordingly He will repay, fury to His adversaries, recompense to His enemies; the coastlands He will fully repay. So shall they fear the name of the LORD from the west, and His glory from the rising of the sun; when the enemy comes in like a flood, the Spirit of the LORD will lift up a standard against him. Isaiah 59:15–19a (NKJV)

By Christine

Years ago, I had a new boss. He and I would argue and fight, almost daily. It was to the point that I almost quit. Every day I was asking God to change him, to make him easier to work with, or leave. It was not until I stopped praying that, and started to pray, "God change me so he can see you and not me!" that the prayer worked. After a few weeks we were like good old friends. I had changed. I let Jesus be the eyes I saw him through. Instead of praying for his downfall, I prayed for his salvation. My attitude changed. I didn't see him as my enemy, but as a child of God, just as I am.

Journaling Exercise

1. List your enemies on a prayer list and pray daily for them.

2. Write down how God is answering your prayers.

Depart from evil, and do good; seek peace, and pursue it.
Psalm 34:14 (KJV)

Lesson 12
FORGIVING TRANSGRESSIONS

orgiving someone that has wronged you will be easier if you compare it to how Jesus sacrificed His *life* so that your sins might be forgiven. By holding on to these feelings of unforgiveness, you are withholding blessings from yourself. The enemy would like nothing better than to have the root of bitterness take hold and consume you until your life feels meaningless.

You cannot move forward in your walk with Christ if you are stuck in the past. When you truly accept that you are a sinner and Jesus is your Redeemer, you will realize that your wounds that were inflicted deep in your soul were suffered as His pains. Lay them at the foot of the cross. Ask Jesus to give you a heart to forgive. It might take many days of praying "I forgive___ for____" until it melts from your heart. God is merciful and He will convict you of the need to forgive when it is time. When you are ready, tell this person lovingly that you forgive him or her. We must forgive without conditions; Jesus forgave us while we were still but sinners.

It is important to grasp the depths of how much God has forgiven you for your debt. We are all but dirty rags; made clean by the blood of Jesus. Have mercy on others, as your Father has mercy on you. In Luke 7, the woman who wept tears on Jesus' feet and poured perfume over them was forgiven much because she loved Him much. The same passage tells us that he who is forgiven little loves little. Understanding how much you were forgiven will open your heart to love more!

Heavenly Father, I pray that You will speak to me through Your Word and provide divine understanding of Your truth. Give me ears to hear and eyes to see and a heart to understand. In Jesus' name I pray, amen.

> **Speak and act as those who are going to be judged by the law that gives freedom, because judgment without mercy will be shown to anyone who has not been merciful. Mercy triumphs over judgment!** *James 2:12–13*
>
> **Make every effort to live in peace with all men and to be holy; without holiness no one will see the Lord. See to it that no one misses the grace of God and that no bitter root grows up to cause trouble and defile many.** *Hebrews 12:14*
>
> **[Jesus said] "Do you see this woman? I came into your house. You did not give me any water for my feet, but she wet my feet with her tears and wiped them with her hair. You did not give me a kiss, but this woman, from the time I entered, has not stopped kissing my feet. You did not put oil on my head, but she has poured perfume on my feet. Therefore I tell you, her many sins have been forgiven—for she loved much. But he who has been forgiven little loves little."** *Luke 7:44–47*

Our goal of forgiveness should be the same as Jesus' goal: reconciliation and restoration of the relationship. Sometimes it will be an immediate reconciliation and other times it will not. It is always in God's timing and His providence. We must do our part to forgive and give all the pain that was caused to the Lord. Your act of forgiveness is a seed for God to water and grow in the heart of the other person.

> **[Jesus said] "And when you stand praying, if you hold anything against anyone, forgive him, so that our Father in heaven may forgive you your sins."** *Mark 11:25*
>
> **Get rid of all bitterness, rage, and anger, brawling and slander, along with every form of malice. Be kind and compassionate to one another, forgiving each other, just as in Christ God forgave you.** *Ephesians 4:31–32*

"Pray, then, in this way: 'Our Father who is in heaven, hallowed be Your name. Your kingdom come. Your will be done, on earth as it is in heaven. Give us this day our daily bread. And forgive us our debts, as we also have forgiven our debtors. And do not lead us into temptation, but deliver us from evil. [For Yours is the kingdom and the power and the glory forever. Amen.]' For if you forgive others for their transgressions, your heavenly Father will also forgive you. But if you do not forgive others, then your Father will not forgive your transgressions." Matthew 6:9–15 (NASB)

If you were hurt deeply as a child or a victim as an adult and feel horror, shame and/or disgrace, God wants your blessings to be a double portion because He hates injustice and iniquity. Your Heavenly Father is your defender and declares that vengeance is His alone. Only He knows what the outcome will be. Verbally confess your deep pain to a trusted sister or brother in Christ and bring these pictures out of the dark recesses of your mind and into the light of day. Pray together for Jesus to heal your pain. Ask Him to replace these bad thoughts with lovely thoughts and for His peace that surpasses all understanding to be upon you. Give your pain to God, and receive a harvest of blessings.

Instead of their shame my people will receive a double portion, and instead of disgrace they will rejoice in their inheritance; and so they will inherit a double portion in their land, and everlasting joy will be theirs. For I, the Lord, love justice; I hate robbery and iniquity. In my faithfulness I will reward them and make an everlasting covenant with them. Isaiah 61:7–8

A key concept that the devil does not want you to know is that he uses people in your life to attack you. Jesus revealed this to me when I needed to forgive someone. When working through the process of forgiving a person who has committed a horrible, unspeakably evil act against you, it is important to rationally see that they do not know Jesus intimately or maybe not at all. If they did, then they would not have committed the act. Because they do not have a personal relationship with

Jesus, they can become easy prey to be a weapon for the devil to use against you. Try to see them as a person who is sick and in need of medicine. The only cure is Jesus. Pray that they find Jesus and are healed.

As Roman soldiers cast lots for Jesus' clothes as He was being crucified, Jesus asked His Father to forgive them, "for they know not what they do." Forgive this person that wronged you, for they know not what they do. Pray also that what man meant for evil, God will use it for good.

> *Then said Jesus, "Father, forgive them; for they know not what they do."* Luke 23:34a (KJV)
>
> *Then his brothers also went and fell down before his face, and they said, "Behold, we are your servants." Joseph said to them, "Do not be afraid, for am I in the place of God? But as for you, <u>you meant evil against me; but God meant it for good</u>, in order to bring it about as it is this day, to save many people alive."* Genesis 50:18–20 (NKJV)
>
> *And we know that in all things God works for the good of those who love him, who have been called according to his purpose.* Romans 8:28

Only Jesus can wash away our pain and make us whiter than snow.

> *Cleanse me with hyssop, and I will be clean; wash me, and I will be whiter than snow. Let me hear joy and gladness; let the bones you have crushed rejoice. Hide your face from my sins and blot out all my iniquity. Create in me a pure heart, O God, and renew a steadfast spirit within me.* Psalm 51:7–10

Sometimes we need to forgive a fellow Christian. One time I had been hurt by a believer and my first reaction was silence and then later I was critical, or judgmental, of her harsh words and what I perceived as an immature Christian. I knew that I needed to forgive her. That very night, I was convicted by God that I needed to see this woman as He saw her in the future, which was beautiful. I also needed to see her through the loving eyes of Jesus. It has taken awhile, but I have seen her heart softening and humility has come over her as God is convicting her.

Our daily prayer should include asking God to give us the eyes of Jesus as we look at others. The Lord knows we all need help with that.

> *For by the grace given to me I say to every one of you: Do not think of yourself more highly than you ought, but rather think of yourself with sober judgment, in accordance with the measure of faith God has given you. Just as each of us has one body with many members, and these members do not all have the same function, so in Christ we who are many form one body with many members, and these members do not all have the same function, so in Christ we who are many form one body, and each member belongs to all the others. Romans 12:3–5*

Prayer of Forgiveness

Lord Jesus, give me Your heart of forgiveness. Melt away this heart that has turned to stone for some people and give me a heart of flesh. Give me Your eyes to see them as You see them and Your love to forgive them. On my own I can never be righteous. Thank you for imparting Your righteousness in me and giving me the need to seek peace out of love. Convict me of whom I need to forgive. In Your precious name I pray, amen.

Journaling Exercise

1. Who do you need to forgive? If they do not know Jesus, pray that they might come to know Him.

2. Write your experiences.

WEEK 3
GROUP QUESTIONS

1. Why does God want us to pray for our enemies?

2. Explain why we have to forgive. If any of you have someone you need to forgive, say their name, and lift them up in prayer. If you would like to share a story, do so with agreement that it is in confidentiality. Remember that when you bring things in your life out of the dark and into the light, you can be released from this power of darkness.

Week 4

GOD'S LOVE

*Trust in Him at all times, O people; Pour out
your hearts before Him; God is a refuge for us.*
Psalm 62:8 (NASB)

Lesson 13
ACCEPTING GOD'S LOVE

God loves you unconditionally and with a perfect "agape love"— a pure, unchangeable love. That is why He willingly sent His beloved Son to die for you. He loves you just the way you are with all your imperfections. If you never did one more thing, He would love you the same. Rest in knowing that you are fully loved and nothing you do can diminish His love. He does not want you to run around frantically trying to please Him with your works. This will only wear you out and make you less useful to Him. You do not have to prove anything to Him, because what His Son did was enough. Jesus put on our robe (our dirty rags) so that we might be clothed in His robe of righteousness. When Jesus died on the cross, He said, "It is finished."

Love God; bask in His love, feel His love raining down on you, rest in His loving hands. Once you begin to rest in His love, you will become renewed, and out of the abundance of His love, you will then be asked to do works for Him. Anything that He asks you to do will then be under His grace and guidance. "There will be inconveniences to bear, self-pleasing to be laid aside along with sacrifices and pain" but what a blessed reward He has in store for you. ("Come Away My Beloved" by Francis J. Roberts)

Heavenly Father, I pray that You will speak to me through Your Word and provide divine understanding of Your truth. Give me ears to hear and eyes to see and a heart to understand. In Jesus' name I pray, amen.

There is no fear in love. But perfect love drives out fear, because fear has to do with punishment. The one who fears is not made perfect in love. We love him, because he first loved us. 1 John 4:18–19

[Jesus said] "For God so loved the world that he gave his only begotten Son, that whosoever believeth in him should not perish, but have everlasting life." John 3:16 (KJV)

Beloved, let us love one another, for love is from God, and whoever loves has been born of God and knows God. Anyone who does not love does not know God, because God is love. In this the love of God was made manifest among us, that God sent his only Son into the world, so that we might live through him. In this is love, not that we have loved God but that he loved us and sent his Son to be the propitiation for our sins. Beloved, if God so loved us, we also ought to love one another. No one has ever seen God; if we love one another, God abides in us and his love is perfected in us. 1 John 4:7–12 (ESV)

I delight greatly in the LORD; my soul rejoices in my God. For he has clothed me with garments of salvation and arrayed me in a robe of righteousness, as a bridegroom adorns his head like a priest, and as a bride adorns herself with her jewels. Isaiah 61:10

I had to learn the hard way to accept God's love. I suffered through the sadness of 13 miscarriages with many of these afterwards having medical procedures where my knees knocked together in fear on the hospital bed. My husband was always there but could not comfort my fear or sadness. God knows he suffered too. For the first seven years of our marriage I knew how it felt to go to baby showers childless. In a 20-year period, in addition to the miscarriages, I had four surgeries to correct a deformed uterus, blood issues, a hernia operation, six trips to the E.R., and a heart surgery to correct an electrical defect. It was only during the last two surgeries that I fully felt God's love pour down on me. He prompted so many people to pray for me. As I was being wheeled into surgery I had no fear and was completely resting in His loving hands. His love truly brings a peace that surpasses all understanding. This peace is attained when we love and trust Him. We love Him, because He first loved us.

Most of my life I have felt that I was not worthy of God's love. As a child I was very sweet, quiet, and sensitive. I remember at an early age the first couple of times I witnessed evil on the screen and was actually shocked and mortified that it existed. I sobbed long after the movies ended. The wickedness of this world and principalities of darkness took their toll on me and I slowly lost my sweetness and it was replaced with a great fear of evil, sadness, guilt, pride, and a need to try to control everything. I desperately missed the feeling I had as a child of being purer of heart. Over time, as my heart became broken over and over, I almost lost the ability to feel love or to accept love from others.

God never stopped loving me and pursuing me. I know now that He truly loves me and was always there through all my suffering and stubbornness. He gave me my fighting spirit and a dog named Rawney that was my faithful companion glued to my side day and night. He directed me to the doctors I needed to be able to have children. God gave me the desires of my heart when we finally had our two children, one through a surrogate and one out of my body. He provided a beautiful Christian lady to carry our son and my largest commissioned account by far to pay for it. God showed me that in my own will I climbed many mountains that I could have easily gone around had I just accepted His love and followed Him. Jesus has shown me how to love, and it is amazing how much love wells up in your heart when you ask His love in.

I will sprinkle clean water on you and you will be clean; I will cleanse you from all your impurities and from all your idols. I will give you a new heart and put a new spirit in you: I will remove from you your heart of stone, and give you a heart of flesh. Ezekiel 36:25–26

The most amazing thing is that my deformed uterus and heart defect were knitted together in my mother's womb by God. He knew it would take these two maladies to finally make me stop trying to be in charge and to accept His love. I was made perfect in His image. You were made perfect in His image. We have to go through trials and suffering in order that we might finally, fully surrender to His design and accept His unfailing love. God desires our whole heart and many times it is completely broken before we finally surrender it to Him.

For you created my inmost being; you knit me together in my mother's womb. I praise you because I am fearfully and wonderfully made; your works are wonderful, I know that full well. My frame was not hidden from you when I was made in the secret place. When I was woven together in the depths of the earth, your eyes saw my unformed body. All the days ordained for me were written in your book before one of them came to be. Psalm 139:13–16

All beautiful you are, my darling; there is no flaw in you. Song of Songs 4:7

The LORD your God in your midst, The Mighty One, will save; he will rejoice over you with gladness, he will quiet you with His love, he will rejoice over you with singing. Zephaniah 3:17(NKJV)

Give thanks to the God of heaven. His love endures forever. Psalm 136:26

Shame from my past had made me feel that I was not worthy of God's love. This is simply not true. We must draw near to God and accept His great love for us. He loves me! He loves you!

Heavenly Father,

Though I was but a sinner, You sought me out. You knew me before I was born, and You created me to know You and to be loved by You. In all my wretchedness, You still loved me. Though I was undeserving, You sent Your Son down to earth. Jesus was beaten, mocked, cursed, and forsaken to give me a way back to You. You so loved the world that You gave Your only Begotten Son.

Thank you for the cross. Thank you for Your great Love. I love You because You first loved me. Help me to know You more, to hear You more, to see You more and to love you more each day. In Jesus' precious name I pray, amen.

Journaling Exercise

1. Please listen online to "Sweetly Broken" by Jeremy Riddle and "How He Loves" by David Crowder Band.

2. Write a thank you letter to God accepting His great love for you. Let Him speak to you as you write. His love will show through!

When I look at your heavens, the work of your fingers, the moon and the stars, which you have set in place, what is man that you are mindful of him, and the son of man that you care for him?
Psalm 8:3–4 (ESV)

Lesson 14
HE LOVES US

God loves us and wants what is best for us. He loves us so much that sometimes we have to learn the hard way in order to receive His best. When we stumble and continue to sin, God, our Father, will discipline us like a beloved son or daughter. If God didn't care, He would let us do whatever we wanted. There is a reason why we are to look at our salvation with fear and trembling. We have to give God His proper place and that would be sitting on the throne in our life. Remember when you were a kid and your mother said, "Just wait until your father gets home!" The same kind of fear and trembling! We should have a good fear of displeasing God and if we continue to keep doing what we know is bad, to expect some discipline. He wants us to improve and prosper and to expect that He will see us through the good work He began in us. It is with this hope that we get through everything to His glory.

Heavenly Father, I pray that You will speak to me through Your Word and provide divine understanding of Your truth. Give me ears to hear and eyes to see and a heart to understand. In Jesus' name I pray, amen.

And you have forgotten that word of encouragement that addresses you as sons: "My son, do not make light of the Lord's discipline, and do not lose heart when he rebukes you, because the Lord disciplines those he loves, and he punishes everyone he accepts as a son." *Hebrews 12:5–6*

The fear of the LORD is the beginning of knowledge, but fools despise wisdom and discipline. Proverbs 1:7

He will be the sure foundation for your times, a rich store of salvation and wisdom and knowledge; the fear of the LORD is the key to this treasure. Isaiah 33:6

Let all the earth fear the Lord; let all the inhabitants of the world stand in awe of Him. For He spoke, and it was done; He commanded, and it stood fast. The LORD nullifies the counsel of the nations; He frustrates the plans of the peoples. The counsel of the LORD stands forever, The plans of His heart from generation to generation. Blessed is the nation whose God is the LORD, the people whom He has chosen for His own inheritance. Psalm 33:8–12 (NASB)

Besides this, we have had earthly fathers who disciplined us and we respected them. Shall we not much more be subject to the Father of spirits and live? For they disciplined us for a short time as it seemed best to them, but he disciplines us for our good, that we may share his holiness. For the moment all discipline seems painful rather than pleasant, but later it yields the peaceful fruit of righteousness to those who have been trained by it. Therefore lift your drooping hands and strengthen your weak knees, and make straight paths for your feet, so that what is lame may not be put out of joint but rather be healed. Hebrews 12:9–13 (ESV)

"For I know the plans I have for you," declares the LORD, "plans to prosper you and not to harm you, plans to give you hope and a future." Jeremiah 29:11

Being confident of this, that he who began a good work in you will carry it on to completion until the day of Christ Jesus. Philippians 1:6

I have a funny personal story of God's discipline. I had a very bad habit of yelling at my husband in the car because he would look one way and then the car would veer out of his lane. God had been convicting me over and over that I needed to stop the criticism. Well, I felt that it was wrong, but the words continued out of my mouth. After an episode where my husband darted across the road to a gas station with a few feet to spare from an oncoming car, I began the rampage. I looked down at my phone on the floor and it had speed dialed the voicemail of a hotel manager in charge of a landscape design project I had been trying to get. I tried desperately to push the button to delete the message but it was too late. Instantly I knew God was telling me that I was going to have to pay the hard way—sheer humiliation. The next day I got a message from the manager that she would not be in need of my services. I have since gotten <u>much</u> better in the car! (So has his driving, go figure…)

God is so much more patient with us than we deserve. He began convicting me that I was driving too fast and impatient with slow drivers for at least a couple of years. One Sunday I was going to pick up someone to take them to church, no less, and I was impatient with the slow driver in front of me. I took a look at their bumper sticker and it read, "Grace Happens." Funny, huh? Well, that was not enough of a conviction for me and I went back to being in a hurry. Months later, I was driving and thinking about what I needed to do next and was not paying attention as I went around a bend. Lo and behold, lights whipped around the street and pulled me over. The officer wrote the ticket for exactly the speed I was going, no niceties, handed me a ticket for $195 and information for a seven-hour traffic school. I thought, "I hope he feels bad." My next thought was that I probably deserved it.

The very next morning I opened up my Bible without thinking and landed in Romans 13, "Submission to Authority." This chapter tells us that "Everyone must submit himself to the governing authorities, for there is no authority except that which God has established." It also says, "Therefore, it is necessary to submit to the authorities, not only because of possible punishment but also because of conscience." Lesson learned. I'm going to obey the speed limit (within 5 mph), show more grace to other drivers, and respect those in authority over me. Thanks, Father.

I don't know about you, but I find that the behaviors that I am the worst at are also where I most frequently judge others. What I do not like to see in my children or others, if I am honest, is what I dislike the most about myself. God wants us to be very careful to examine and correct our own behavior before pointing out behaviors in others. It is at this point humility sets in.

"Do not judge so that you will not be judged. For in the way you judge, you will be judged; and by your standard of measure, it will be measured to you. Why do you look at the speck that is in your brother's eye, but do not notice the log that is in your own eye? Or how can you say to your brother, 'Let me take the speck out of your eye,' and behold, the log is in your own eye? You hypocrite, first take the log out of your own eye, and then you will see clearly to take the speck out of your brother's eye." Matthew 7:1–5 (NASB)

You, therefore, have no excuse, you who pass judgment on someone else, for at whatever point you judge the other, you are condemning yourself, because you who pass judgment do the same things. Now we know that God's judgment against those who do such things is based on truth. So when you a mere man, pass judgment on them and yet do the same things, do you think you will escape God's judgment? Romans 2:1–2

King David was said to have a heart for God, yet he did horrible acts, including committing adultery with Bathsheba and then having her husband killed in order to have her for himself. What David did have was a deep sorrow for his actions and a repentant heart. A repentant heart means to ask for forgiveness for a fault and then turn away from this behavior and turn towards Jesus and emulate what He would do. If God is convicting you to change a behavior, repent, and get right with God. We cannot just feel convicted over and over, but actually get down on our knees and repent. You will feel joy afterwards.

[Psalm of David] Against you, you only, have I sinned and done what is evil in your sight, so that you are proved right when you speak and justified when you judge. Surely I was sinful at birth, sinful from the time my mother conceived me. Surely you desire truth in the inner parts; you teach me wisdom in the inmost place. Cleanse me with hyssop, and I will be clean; wash me, and I will be whiter than snow. Psalm 51:4–7

Godly sorrow brings repentance that leads to salvation and leaves no regret, but worldly sorrow brings death. 2 Corinthians 7:10

Produce fruit in keeping with repentance. Matthew 3:8

The example Jesus gave of not being condemned for our sins was the woman who had been caught in adultery. Jesus asked that anyone that was without sin could throw the first stone. No one could condemn her and neither did Jesus. He forgave her and told her to go and sin no more.

When we repent of our sins, Jesus wants us to stop doing them. It is so easy to slip back into our old ways, our old selves. Repent and ask Jesus for His resurrection power to renew us and help us. We may stumble, but Jesus never will. Each day can be a new start for our new self. God's mercy is new each morning!

Jesus Christ is the same yesterday and today and forever. Hebrews 13:8
The steadfast love of the LORD never ceases; his mercies never come to an end; they are new every morning; great is your faithfulness. Lamentations 3:22 (ESV)

God's discipline is not punishment like lightning, but rather His deep love for us that desires us to be holy. Praise God that we are worthy of His refining! He loves us.

Journaling Exercise

1. Please listen online to "Good Good Father" by Chris Tomlin.
2. What is God convicting you to change? If you need to, get down on your knees in godly sorrow, repent, and receive God's grace. We need to ask Jesus to help us become more like Him and turn from our wicked ways. We are weak, but He is strong.

When I thought, "My foot slips," your steadfast love, O LORD held me up.
When the cares of my heart are many, your consolations cheer my soul.
Psalm 94:18 (ESV)

Lesson 15

Cast Your Anxiety on the LORD

Anxiety and fears are emotions that everyone faces almost on a daily basis if we don't go to God. We must remember how faithful God is to us and we must have great faith in Him. Fear equals little faith. God did not give us a spirit of fear, but of power, and love, and a sound mind. If you are fearful about a situation, say to yourself: "Perfect love casts out all fear," and think of Jesus' perfect love on the cross. Imagine His blood pouring over you on the cross to calm your fear.

We receive things according to our faith. Remember that every good and perfect gift comes from our heavenly Father. When we allow fear to take hold, then we are blocking God's blessings and letting the devil reign in our lives. It actually can start with pride in thinking that we have to fix everything ourselves.

Proverbs 16:18 tells us that "pride goes before destruction, a haughty spirit before a fall." Pride is a sin. When we are prideful, sin enters and this allows an open doorway for the devil to bring in fear and anxiety of what is to become of us. If there is an issue of pride in your life, then command your thoughts captive to the obedience of Jesus Christ and slam the door on the enemy. The enemy will give up after a while. We must live in faith that our mighty God is in control, not us, and He will see us through until the very day we die and see our beloved Jesus.

When you are overwhelmed with a situation, begin to praise God. Praise Him in the storm. Sing songs of praise. Find strength and refuge in God alone. If the only words you can cry out are "Abba, (Daddy) Help me!", then He will comfort you. Cast your anxieties on the LORD, and see what miracle He brings forth.

Heavenly Father, I pray that You will speak to me through Your Word and provide divine understanding of Your truth. Give me ears to hear and eyes to see and a heart to understand. In Jesus' name I pray, amen.

"Therefore I tell you, do not be anxious about your life, what you will eat or what you will drink, nor about your body, what you will put on. Is not life more than food, and the body more than clothing? Look at the birds of the air: they neither sow nor reap nor gather into barns, and yet your heavenly Father feeds them. Are you not of more value than they? And which of you by being anxious can add a single hour to his span of life? And why are you anxious about clothing? Consider the lilies of the field, how they grow: they neither toil nor spin, yet I tell you, even Solomon in all his glory was not arrayed like one of these. But if God so clothes the grass of the field, which today is alive and tomorrow is thrown into the oven, will he not much more clothe you, O you of little faith? Therefore do not be anxious, saying, 'What shall we eat?' or 'What shall we drink?' or 'What shall we wear?' For the Gentiles seek after all these things, and your heavenly Father knows that you need them all. But seek first the kingdom of God and his righteousness, and all these things will be added to you. "Therefore do not be anxious about tomorrow, for tomorrow will be anxious for itself. Sufficient for the day is its own trouble." Matthew 6:25–34 (ESV)

Humble yourselves, therefore, under God's mighty hand, that he may lift you up in due time. Cast all your anxiety on him because he cares for you. 1 Peter 5:6–7

You will keep in perfect peace him whose mind is steadfast, because he trusts in you. Trust in the LORD forever, for the LORD, the LORD, is the Rock eternal. Isaiah 26:3–4

Every good and perfect gift is from above, coming down from the Father of the heavenly lights, who does not change like shifting shadows. James 1:17

Commit your work to the LORD, and your plans will be established. Proverbs 16:3 (ESV)

…If God is for us, who can be against us? He who did not spare his own Son, but gave him up for us all—how will he not also, along with him, graciously give us all things? Romans 8:31–32

[Jesus said] "Are not five sparrows sold for two copper coins? And not one of them is forgotten before God. But the very hairs of your head are all numbered. Do not fear therefore; you are of more value than many sparrows." Luke 12: 6–7 (NKJV)

So do not fear, for I am with you; do not be dismayed, for I am your God. I will strengthen you and help you; I will uphold you with my righteous right hand. Isaiah 41:10

I used to have a great fear of going over bridges. I know that the enemy gave this to me because before I married a Christian, I had no problem driving over the Golden Gate Bridge on a regular basis. Once I married my husband, I would literally have an anxiety attack when I went over a tall bridge and would slow down to almost a stop on a few occasions. It was all I could do to will myself to keep driving.

On a trip through Portland I was driving with my daughter in the backseat. I saw that I was going to have to cross over a very long, curved bridge. I couldn't handle the thought. Finally, I prayed, "Jesus, I cannot take this fear any more. You have to take it from me." Guess what? He took it from me! As I went over that bridge, all I could think of was Jesus walking on the water next to me with His arm stretched out. To this day that is what I think of when I go over a bridge and experience His peace. I am still working on my fear of steep heights while driving through mountains, but I can tell you what helps if you suffer from this: Plead the blood of Jesus over your car and all airways around it.

When anxious, recite these two verses below and then do what they say. In prayer, we must let our requests be known with supplication (asking or begging for something earnestly or humbly), give thanks and ask to receive His peace that surpasses all understanding to guard your heart and mind in Christ Jesus.

Do not be anxious about anything, but in everything by prayer and supplication with thanksgiving let your requests be made known to God. And the peace of God, which surpasses all understanding, will guard your hearts and your minds in Christ Jesus. Philippians 4:6–7 (NKJV)

Jesus understands our fears because He was tempted by fear while He was a man. In the garden of Gethsemane, His sweat was like drops of blood as He thought of what He was about to endure the next day. Jesus fell to the ground in agony and prayed, "My Father, if it is possible, may this cup be taken from me. Yet not as I will, but as you will." Jesus overcame His fears and bravely went to the cross for us. He has mercy on us and that is a comfort in itself.

When the ways of the world get you down, remember Jesus has already overcome the world for us. Jesus loves us and He has our backs. When you pray in the morning, claim the victory of this day because Jesus has already overcome the world for us. We are fighting <u>from</u> His victory; not for it. Always keep your eyes on the prize: Jesus.

"Behold, the hour is coming, indeed it has come, when you will be scattered, each to his own home, and will leave me alone. Yet I am not alone, for the Father is with me. I have said these things to you, that in me you may have peace. In the world you will have tribulation. But take heart; I have overcome the world." John 16:32–33

This is love for God: to obey his commands. And his commands are not burdensome, for everyone born of God overcomes the world. This is the victory that has overcome the world, even our faith. Who is it that overcomes the world? Only he who believes that Jesus is the Son of God. 1 John 5:3–5

Do you not know that in a race all the runners run, but only one gets the prize? Run in such a way as to get the prize. Everyone who competes in the games goes into strict training. They do it to get a crown that will not last; but we do it to get a crown that will last forever. Therefore I do not run like a man running aimlessly; I do not fight like a man beating the air. No, I beat my body and make it my slave so that after I have preached to others, I myself will not be disqualified for the prize. 1 Corinthians 9:24–27

Let us fix our eyes on Jesus, the author and perfecter of our faith, who for the joy set before him, endured the cross, scorning shame, and sat down at the right hand of the throne of God. Hebrews 12:2

Sometimes the battle you are going through might seem too big for you, but you must remember that you serve the Almighty God, Yahweh, who controls the Universe. He will fight the battle, but you must give it to Him and listen for His lead. You are His servant and His beloved child, and *the battle is the LORD'S.* Acknowledge that the battle is the LORD'S, like David did in 1 Samuel, and ask Him to lead you to victory.

[David said to the 9' giant Goliath] All those gathered here will know that it is not by sword or spear that the LORD saves; for the battle is the LORD'S, and he will give all of you into our hands. 1 Samuel 17:47

He said: Listen, King Jehoshaphat and all who live in Judah and Jerusalem! This is what the LORD says to you: 'Do not be afraid or discouraged because of this vast army. <u>For the battle is not yours, but God's</u>. Tomorrow march down against them. They will be climbing up by the Pass of Ziz, and you will find them at the end of the gorge in the Desert of Jeruel. You will not have to fight this battle. Take up your positions; stand firm and see the deliverance the LORD will give you, O Judah and Jerusalem. Do not be afraid; do not be discouraged. Go out to face them tomorrow, and the LORD will be with you'. 2 Chronicles 20:15–17

You give me your shield of victory; you stoop down to make me great. 2 Samuel 22:36

The LORD will fight for you; you need only to be still. Exodus 14:14

Our pastor preached on the passage in Mark about Jesus calming the storm. Jesus asks us to get in the boat and go to the other side. The storm may be raging, but never forget that Jesus is in our boat.

And a great windstorm arose, and the waves beat into the boat, so that it was already filling. But He was in the stern, asleep on a pillow. And they awoke Him and said to Him, "Teacher, do You not care that we are perishing?" Then He arose and rebuked the wind, and said to the sea, "Peace, be still!" And the wind ceased and there was a great calm.
Mark 4:37–39 (NKJV)

A Prayer for an Anxious Heart

Heavenly Father,

Thank you for Your great mercy. I come before You with an anxious heart. In 1 John 5 You reveal that I have the confidence to approach You and if I ask anything that is in accordance to Your will, You hear me. And if I know that You hear me, whatever I ask, I know that I will have what I ask of You.

When Jesus raised Lazarus from the dead, He said, "Father, I thank you that You have heard me." (Tell God what you are anxious about.)

Father, I thank you that You have heard me. This battle is Yours, LORD. I put these issues into Your loving hands. Jesus, I ask You to calm this raging sea in me. You are in control and it is well with my soul.

In Jesus' Holy Name I pray, amen.

Journaling Exercise

1. Write down the eight verses of Psalm 121. Reflect on God's promises.

2. Please listen online to the beautiful song "It Is Well" by Kristene DiMarco & Bethel Music-You Make Me Brave.

Oh, visit me with Your salvation, that I may see the benefit of Your chosen ones, that I may rejoice in the gladness of Your nation, that I may glory with Your inheritance.
Psalm 106:4b–5 (NKJV)

Lesson 16
CHILDREN OF GOD

eace will follow as you walk your path with Jesus and grow as a child of God. You will be in Christ, and He within you. God made a covenant with us that He would write His laws on our hearts and minds and that our sins are forgiven and remembered no more. He cast our sins away as far as the east is from the west. Jesus broke that sin by the blood of the Lamb. You are free of it by His righteousness. This freedom allows us to focus on daily transforming into His image. According to The Open Bible (NASB) there is a threefold proof of this new birth in us. First, there is the inward change when we accept Christ. Second, there is outgoing proof of Christ's love working through us. Finally, outward proof by practicing righteousness through choosing to do what is right at all costs.

Heavenly Father, I pray that You will speak to me through Your Word and provide divine understanding of Your truth. Give me ears to hear and eyes to see and a heart to understand. In Jesus' name I pray, amen.

Yet to all who received him, to those who believed in his name, he gave the right to become children of God—children born not of natural descent, nor of human decision or a husband's will, but born of God. John 1:12–13

[Children of God] See how great a love the Father has bestowed on us, that we would be called children of God; and such we are. For this reason the world does not know us, because it did not know Him.

Beloved, now we are children of God, and it has not appeared as yet what we will be. We know that when He appears, we will be like Him, because we will see Him just as He is. And everyone who has this hope fixed on Him purifies himself, just as He is pure. Everyone who practices sin also practices lawlessness; and sin is lawlessness. You know that He appeared in order to take away sins; and in Him there is no sin. No one who abides in Him sins; no one who sins has seen Him or knows Him. Little children, make sure no one deceives you; the one who practices righteousness is righteous, just as He is righteous; the one who practices sin is of the devil; for the devil has sinned from the beginning. The Son of God appeared for this purpose, to destroy the works of the devil. No one who is born of God practices sin, because His seed abides in him; and he cannot sin, because he is born of God. By this the children of God and the children of the devil are obvious: anyone who does not practice righteousness is not of God, nor the one who does not love his brother. 1 John 3:1–10 (NASB)

But you are a chosen people, a royal priesthood, a holy nation, a people belonging to God, that you may declare the praises of him who called you out of darkness into his wonderful light. Once you were not a people, but now you are the people of God; once you had not received mercy, but now you have received mercy. Dear friends, I urge you, as aliens and strangers in the world, to abstain from sinful desires, which war against your soul. Live such good lives among the pagans that, though they accuse you of doing wrong, they may see your good deeds and glorify God on the day he visits us. 1 Peter 2:9–12

"This is the covenant that I will make with them after those days, says the Lord: I will put My laws upon their heart, and on their mind I will write them." He then says, "And their sins and their lawless deeds I will remember no more." Now where there is forgiveness of these things, there is no longer any offering for sin. Therefore, brethren, since we have confidence to enter the holy place by the blood of Jesus, by a new and living way which He inaugurated for us through the veil, that is, His flesh, and since we have a great priest over the house of God, let us draw

near with a sincere heart in full assurance of faith, having our hearts sprinkled clean from an evil conscience and our bodies washed with pure water. Hebrews 10:16–22 (NASB)

God has adopted us into His family as beloved sons and daughters. He is our Father. He is our Abba, our Daddy. By His grace we have been given a seat at His table. He loves us, takes care of us, encourages us, gives us precious gifts, and wants what is best for us as only the perfect Father can. Not only are we His sons and daughters who receive freedom from our bondages, but we are co-heirs with Christ and look forward to receiving our full inheritance when Jesus returns in glory. Claim your inheritance the next time the devil tries to condemn you!

For you did not receive a spirit that makes you a slave again to fear, but you received the Spirit of sonship. And by him we cry, "Abba, Father." The Spirit himself testifies with our spirit that we are God's children. Now if we are children, then we are heirs—heirs of God and co-heirs with Christ, if indeed we share in his sufferings in order that we may also share in his glory. Romans 8:15–17

Or what man is there among you who, when his son asks for a loaf, will give him a stone? Or if he asks for a fish, he will not give him a snake, will he? If you then, being evil, know how to give good gifts to your children, how much more will your Father who is in heaven give what is good to those who ask Him! Matthew 7:9–11 (NASB)

The creation waits in eager expectation for the sons of God to be revealed. For the creation was subjected to frustration, not by its own choice, but by the will of the one who subjected it, in hope that the creation itself will be liberated from its bondage to decay and brought into the glorious freedom of the children of God. Romans 8: 19–21

Because you are sons, God sent the Spirit of his Son into our hearts, the Spirit who calls out, "Abba, Father." So you are no longer a slave, but a son; and since you are a son, God has made you also an heir. Galatians 4:6–7

Journaling Exercise

1. Please listen online to "No Longer Slaves" by Jonathan David and Melissa Helser (Bethel Music).

2. Where are you in your walk with Christ? Do you have inward proof, outgoing proof, and outward proof that you are growing in Christ?

WEEK 4
GROUP QUESTIONS

1. Who has had a hard time feeling worthy of God's love? Pray for the love of God to be revealed to them.

2. What did it take for you to accept God's unconditional, agape love for you?

3. Does anyone have an example of God's discipline in their life?

4. What anxieties do you need to cast on the LORD? Pray for each other and give these battles over to the LORD.

5. What does it mean to be a child of God?

Week 5

WALK BY FAITH

Make me to know your ways, O LORD; teach me your paths. Lead me in your truth and teach me, for you are the God of my salvation; for you I wait all the day long.

Psalm 25:4–5 (ESV)

Lesson 17

LIVE BY FAITH, NOT THE LAW

When we believe that Jesus is the Son of God and rose on the third day, we (Gentiles) are grafted into the Olive Tree of God's chosen people, with Abraham being the father of us all. Abraham believed God's covenant with him that his offspring would be as numerous as the stars, that God would give the land between the river of Egypt and the Euphrates River to his descendants, and that he would be the father of many nations. Even though Abraham was old, his wife was barren, and he had waited 25 years for his son to be born, he believed what God told him. And his faith was counted as righteousness.

As Christians, God made a covenant with us, and we believe that our sins have been forgiven and we have been justified by the blood of Jesus. Our righteous standing with God comes from faith in Jesus Christ alone. It cannot come from us. It is not by works. We have faith that Christ's sacrifice was enough. Charles Spurgeon in his book, *All of Grace*, defines faith as: knowledge, belief, and trust. First we hear, then we believe, and then we put our trust in our heavenly Father.

Heavenly Father, I pray that You will speak to me through Your Word and provide divine understanding of Your truth. Give me ears to hear and eyes to see and a heart to understand. In Jesus' name I pray, amen.

For the promise to Abraham or to his descendants that he would be heir of the world was not through the Law, but through the righteousness of faith. For if those who are of the Law are heirs, faith is made void and

the promise is nullified; for the Law brings about wrath, but where there is no law, there also is no violation. For this reason it is by faith, in order that it may be in accordance with grace, so that the promise will be guaranteed to all the descendants, not only to those who are of the Law, but also to those who are of the faith of Abraham, who is the father of us all. Romans 4:13–16 (NASB)

But the Scripture declares that the whole world is a prisoner of sin, so that what was promised, being given through faith in Jesus Christ, might be given to those who believe. Before this faith came, we were held prisoners by the law, locked up until faith should be revealed. So the law was put in charge to lead us to Christ that we might be justified by faith. Galatians 3:22–24

For in the gospel a righteousness from God is revealed, a righteousness that is by faith from first to last, just as it is written: "The righteous will live by faith." Romans 1:17

You who are trying to be justified by the law have been alienated from Christ; you have fallen away from grace. But by faith we eagerly await through the Spirit the righteousness for which we hope. Galatians 5:4–5

For it is by grace you have been saved, through faith—and this not from yourselves, it is the gift of God—not by works, so that no one can boast. For we are God's workmanship, created in Christ Jesus to do good works, which God prepared in advance for us to do. Ephesians 2:8–10

The Law was handed down by God to inform people of what was right and wrong. Before that, people did whatever pleased them and had nothing to assess their morality. Once the laws were in place, there was a measurement of God's standards for us. In our sinful nature, we want to test these laws. Paul says in Romans 7, verse 18a, "I know that nothing good lives in me, that is, in my sinful nature." Not one person other than Jesus can say they have always obeyed the Ten Commandments. Even harder still, Jesus gave us additional rules in his Sermon on the Mount. Not only should one not commit adultery, but if one looks at a woman other than his wife with lust, he has committed adultery. Jesus gave us even more difficult rules to follow.

Legalism will never get us to the point of a righteous standing with God. Because we all fall short of the glory of God, we all desperately need the righteousness that transfers to us when we have faith in Jesus Christ. Jesus came to fulfill the Law for us. His love and grace transforms us. Where the law came to inform, Jesus came to transform by the renewal of our hearts and minds.

I have been crucified with Christ and I no longer live, but Christ lives in me. The life I live in the body, I live by faith in the Son of God, who loved me and gave himself for me. I do not set aside the grace of God, for if righteousness could be gained through the law, Christ died for nothing! Galatians 2:20–21

For the law was given through Moses; grace and truth came through Jesus Christ. John 1:17 (ESV)

For in my inner being I delight in God's law; but I see another law at work in the members of my body, waging war against the law of my mind and making me a prisoner of the law of sin at work within my members. What a wretched man I am! Who will rescue me from this body of death? Thanks be to God—through Jesus Christ our Lord! Romans 7:22–25

Do not be conformed to this world, but be transformed by the renewal of your mind, that by testing you may discern what is the will of God, what is good and acceptable and perfect. Romans 12:2 (ESV)

Faith is being sure of what we hope for and certain of what we do not see. Faith is usually a building process. It's pretty rare to wake up and have complete faith. Small children seem to be very good at this. That is why Jesus said we must have the faith of a little child. God uses the trials we go through in life to build our faith. As we look backwards, we see that His hand was upon us and we can draw on these experiences as we face yet another trial.

Our hope comes from God alone. In this hope we need to rest assured that God will do what He promised and will see us through the good work He began in us. He is our refuge and we must trust that He will never leave us or forsake us. Hebrews 11:6 tells us that "without faith it is impossible to please God because anyone who comes to him must believe that he exists and that he rewards those who earnestly seek him."

> *Now faith is the assurance of things hoped for, the conviction of things not seen. For by it the people of old received their commendation. By faith we understand that the universe was created by the word of God, so that what is seen was not made out of things that are visible. By faith Abel offered to God a more acceptable sacrifice than Cain, through which he was commended as righteous, God commending him by accepting his gifts.* Hebrews 11:1–4a (ESV)
>
> *By faith Enoch was taken away so that he did not see death, "and was not found, because God had taken him"; for before he was taken he had this testimony, that he pleased God. But without faith it is impossible to please Him, for he who comes to God must believe that He is, and that He is a rewarder of those who diligently seek Him.* Hebrews 11:5–6 (NKJV)
>
> *Though you have not seen him, you love him; and even though you do not see him now, you believe in him and are filled with an inexpressible and glorious joy, for you are receiving the goal of your faith, the salvation of your souls.* 1 Peter 1:8–9
>
> *Find rest, O my soul, in God alone; my hope comes from him. He alone is my rock and my salvation; he is my fortress, I will not be shaken. My salvation and my honor depend on God; he is my mighty rock, my refuge. Trust in him at all times, O people; pour out your hearts to him, for God is our refuge.* Psalm 62:5–8
>
> *"Being confident of this, that he who began a good work in you will carry it on to completion until the day of Christ Jesus."* Philippians 1:6
>
> *If God is for us, who can be against us?* Romans 8:31b (NKJV)

Faith is a heavenly gift that Christ sustains. Ask Jesus to increase your faith. Charles Spurgeon (edited by Jim Reimann) wrote in "Morning By Morning" that "Christ Jesus is so delighted with the heavenly gift of faith that he never ceases to strengthen and sustain her…"

The grace of our Lord was poured out on me abundantly along with the faith and love that are in Christ Jesus. 1 Timothy 1:14

Prayer of Faith

Heavenly Father, I pray for the faith of Abraham. His faith was so strong that he was willing to sacrifice his own son in obedience to You. I struggle at times to give my whole heart, trusting that You are in control. Please help my unbelief so that my faith is pure and unshaken. Jesus said in Mark 9:23 that "everything is possible for him who believes." To this, the father of the possessed boy responded, "Lord, I believe, help my unbelief."

Lord, I believe, help my unbelief. Help me to increase my faith and trust in You.

Help me to understand that all I need to do is fix my eyes on You, Jesus, for as it is written, You alone are "the author and perfecter of our faith" (Hebrews 12:2). Please fill me with your love.

Thank you for Your goodness, Thank you for Your grace. In Jesus' mighty name I pray, amen.

Journaling Exercise

1. Please listen online to "Trust in You" by Lauren Daigle.
2. Describe the trials in your life where faith was needed.

3. What did God do when He answered your prayer for help?

The LORD is my portion; I have promised to keep Your words.
Psalm 119:57(NASB)

Lesson 18

BAPTISM

nce you have professed Jesus as your Lord and Savior, get baptized in obedience as a public profession of your faith and commitment to Christ. If you have been baptized but do not feel you did it with the right consciousness, get baptized again. We will never be worthy enough, just know that Jesus commands us to be baptized. The Bible instructs us to repent for the forgiveness of our sins, be baptized, and receive the Holy Spirit. Repent means to turn away from your fight for control and turn toward Jesus and give Him control. Baptism is an outward expression of an inward change. As you go down in the water it symbolizes the death of Christ and as you rise up out of the water, it symbolizes the resurrection of Christ and your good conscience to God. Jesus showed us how to be baptized when He was fully immersed by John the Baptist and the Holy Spirit descended on Him like a dove.

Heavenly Father, I pray that You will speak to me through Your Word and provide divine understanding of Your truth. Give me ears to hear and eyes to see and a heart to understand. In Jesus' name I pray, amen.

> **And Jesus came up and spoke to them, saying, "All authority has been given to Me in heaven and on earth. Go therefore and make disciples of all the nations, baptizing them in the name of the Father and the Son and the Holy Spirit, teaching them to observe all that I commanded you; and lo, I am with you always, even to the end of the age."** *Matthew 28:18–20 (NASB)*

[Speaking of Noah] In it only a few people, eight in all, were saved through water, and this water symbolizes baptism that now saves you also—not the removal of dirt from the body but the pledge of a good conscience toward God. It saves you by the resurrection of Jesus Christ, who has gone into heaven and is at God's right hand—with angels, authorities and power in submission to him. 1 Peter 3:20b–22

And He said to them, "Go into all the world and preach the gospel to all creation. He who has believed and has been baptized shall be saved; but he who has disbelieved shall be condemned. Mark 16:15–16 (NASB)

Or do you not know that all of us who have been baptized into Christ Jesus have been baptized into His death? Therefore we have been buried with Him through baptism into death, so that as Christ was raised from the dead through the glory of the Father, so we too might walk in newness of life. Romans 6:3–4 (NASB)

Peter said to them, "Repent, and each of you be baptized in the name of Jesus Christ for the forgiveness of your sins; and you will receive the gift of the Holy Spirit." Acts 2:38 (NASB)

But John [the Baptist] tried to prevent Him, saying, "I have need to be baptized by You, and do You come to me?" But Jesus answering said to him, "Permit it at this time; for in this way it is fitting for us to fulfill all righteousness." Then he permitted Him. After being baptized, Jesus came up immediately from the water; and behold, the heavens were opened, and he saw the Spirit of God descending as a dove and lighting on Him, and behold, a voice out of the heavens said, "This is My beloved Son, in whom I am well-pleased." Matthew 3:14–17 (NASB)

My husband accepted the Lord with great enthusiasm at the age of 12. He was on fire for the Lord and read his Bible front to back many times through his teenage years, but he was never baptized. As he began college, the ways of the world began to encroach and his Bibles began to collect dust on his bookshelf. His best friend's dad was the pastor who married us with the Word of God. As we began our marriage, my husband was walking away from the Lord as he got caught up in his job and sports and I was on my way to walking towards the Lord through my suffering. God knows all. When I accepted the Lord, we were at the same point in our walk and we absorbed the Word of God like a sponge. It was very fitting that we were baptized at the same time.

I can testify how important it is to be baptized by how much our family was under attack from the enemy before my husband and I were to be baptized on a Sunday night. We both were sick and could barely speak and our daughter was running a fever. Everything was against us. I knew we were under attack, so I gave my daughter some fever reducer, we got in the car, and my mother-in-law kept watch over her. Both of our voices came back right before the event and when the baptism was over, my daughter was no longer sick. Later, at a different church, my son decided to spontaneously get baptized with others that had been scheduled. Before this service, he was having fits of anger and adamantly did not want to go to church. The enemy does not want you to get baptized because his power is diminished and yours is increased greatly.

Journaling Exercise
1. Write of your experience when you were baptized.

2. If you haven't been baptized, what is keeping you from this gift? If you feel God prompting that it is time to get baptized, look ahead to Lesson 30: Baptized by Fire.

I will praise You, O Lord my God, with all my heart,
And I will glorify your name forevermore.
Psalm 86:12 (NKJV)

Lesson 19

GLORIFY THE LORD

When the Holy Spirit was convicting me about changing my thoughts and words, over and over through the night I heard in my sleep, "Glorify the Lord." What does it mean to glorify the Lord? God has shown me that we must glorify Him with our praises, our thoughts and words, and our acts of obedience. It is easy to get caught up in being proper and rigid because we are so serious about following the rules. What He wants us to do is to be joyful and continually praise Him and receive His grace. By being under His grace, our thoughts, words, and actions naturally begin to change.

First, we must magnify the LORD and exalt His name together. Praise Jesus! Be so thankful that you are not where you used to be. Praise Him for loving you first and seeking you out. Praise Him for all the blessings you have received from Him, and those plans He has still to come for you. Praise our Lord God Almighty in the good times and the bad times.

Heavenly Father, I pray that You will speak to me through Your Word and provide divine understanding of Your truth. Give me ears to hear and eyes to see and a heart to understand. In Jesus' name I pray, amen.

Glorify the LORD with me; let us exalt his name together. *Psalm 34:3*

O LORD, you are my God; I will exalt you and praise your name, for in perfect faithfulness you have done marvelous things, things planned long ago. *Isaiah 25:1*

Make a joyful noise to the LORD, all the earth! Serve the LORD with gladness! Come into his presence with singing! Know that the LORD, he is God! It is he who made us, and we are his; we are his people, and the sheep of his pasture. Enter his gates with thanksgiving, and his courts with praise! Give thanks to him; bless his name! For the LORD is good; his steadfast love endures forever, and his faithfulness to all generations. Psalm 100:1–5 (ESV)

Why are you downcast, O my soul? Why so disturbed within me? Put your hope in God, for I will yet praise him, my Savior and my God. Psalm 42:5–6a

I will praise God's name in song and glorify him with thanksgiving. Psalm 69:30

This is the day the LORD has made; let us rejoice and be glad in it. Psalm 118:24 (ESV)

To him who loves us and has freed us from our sins by his blood, and made us a kingdom, priests to his God and Father, to him be glory and dominion forever and ever. Amen. Revelation 1:5b–6 (ESV)

Second, our thoughts and words should glorify and honor Him. We are called to focus on whatever is true, noble, right, pure, lovely, admirable, excellent, or praiseworthy. (Philippians 4:8) God wants us to get rid of anger, rage, malice, slander, and filthy language. (Ephesians 4:31) We can do this when we call on Jesus for help. Pray often that all of your thoughts and imagination are held captive to the obedience of Jesus Christ. We are called to stop grumbling. Oh how we love to grumble! This was a BIG conviction for me. The Israelites that were rescued out of Egypt wandered in the wilderness for 40 years, in large part because of their grumbling. The sooner we get out of this state the better! We are supposed to "do everything without complaining or arguing, so that you may become blameless and pure, children of God without fault in a crooked and depraved generation, in which you shine like stars in the universe." (Philippians 2:14–15)

Complaining of physical pain and symptoms is one of my worst issues. I am realizing that it is a foothold that the devil uses to keep me suffering. What I am learning to do is to think of everything that is "good, pure, and lovely" when I start to have physical pain. I start recalling scenes of happy memories that God has blessed me with in my life. I think of Jesus and I praise the Lord. I ask for Jesus to heal my pain. My headache or other ailments go away when I do this. The next time you are about to complain start praising the Lord instead and see how much power you receive.

The weapons we fight with are not the weapons of the world. On the contrary, they have divine power to demolish strongholds. We demolish arguments and every pretension that sets itself up against the knowledge of God, and <u>we take captive every thought to make it obedient to Christ.</u> 2 Corinthians 10:4–5

Finally, brother, whatever is true, whatever is noble, whatever is right, whatever is pure, whatever is lovely, whatever is admirable, if anything is excellent or praiseworthy-think about such things. Whatever you have learned or received or heard from me, or seen in me-put it into practice. And the God of peace will be with you. Philippians 4:8–9

You also, be patient. Establish your hearts, for the coming of the Lord is at hand. Do not grumble against one another, brothers, so that you may not be judged. James 5:8–9a (ESV)

The words that we speak have so much power and can be for good or for evil. Before speaking, we must always be mindful that with our tongues we have the power to bring life and healing. We also have the power to bring negativity and death. Claim the power of His word out of your mouth by proclaiming scripture verses. Instead of saying "I feel so old," say, "My youth is renewed like the eagle's." Or, instead of saying "I have a terrible memory now," say "I am transformed by the renewal of my mind." Turn "I can't do this" into "I can do all things through Christ who strengthens me!" God's Word does not return void: it has mighty power.

Focus on positive words coming forth. I do some volunteer work with small children where I am able to say to them, "God made you good, kind, and strong," and watch their attitudes become more positive. They pump their arms to show how strong they are. If they do something that is not nice, I ask them, "Is that kind like Jesus?" As faithful Christians, we all need to focus on speaking words of life and not death. Speak words from heaven and not words from hell.

What has helped me tremendously is to not respond in my sinful nature. If I get a text/message from someone and my first reaction is to be irritated, I do not respond right away. I pray and wait until my response is what Jesus would have me say. It is then out of love and not something I will regret later.

Heavenly Father, I pray that You will speak to me through Your Word and provide divine understanding of Your truth. Give me ears to hear and eyes to see and a heart to understand. In Jesus' name I pray, amen.

May the words of my mouth and the meditation of my heart be pleasing in your sight. *Psalm 19:14*

A soft answer turns away wrath, but a harsh word stirs up anger. The tongue of the wise commends knowledge, but the mouths of fools pour out folly. The eyes of the LORD are in every place, keeping watch on the evil and the good. A gentle tongue is a tree of life, but perverseness in it breaks the spirit. *Proverbs 15:1–4 (ESV)*

There is one who speaks rashly like the thrusts of a sword, But the tongue of the wise brings healing. *Proverbs 12:18 (NASB)*

If anyone thinks he is religious and does not bridle his tongue but deceives his heart, this person's religion is worthless. *James 1:26 (ESV)*

Death and life are in the power of the tongue, and those who love it will eat its fruits. *Proverbs 18:21 (ESV)*

"For as the rain comes down, and the snow from heaven, And do not return there, But water the earth, And make it bring forth and bud, That it may give seed to the sower And bread to the eater, So shall My word be that goes forth from My mouth, It shall not return to Me void, But it shall accomplish what I please, And it shall prosper in the thing for which I sent it." *Isaiah 55:10–11 (NKJV)*

The verse that really convicted me of how much our words matter was Matthew 5:22. In this verse "Raca" translates as calling someone a "dummy" and saying "You fool" can put you in danger of the fire of hell. We have all said much worse than this.

[Jesus said] But I tell you that anyone who is angry with his brother will be subject to judgment. Again, anyone who says to his brother, 'Raca,' is answerable to the Sanhedrin. But anyone who says 'You fool!' will be in danger of the fire of hell. Matthew 5:22

The Bible instructed us to listen more and to speak less. We have two ears and only one mouth; I have heard the advice to "Listen twice and speak once." It is very helpful to pray that God might make your thoughts, His thoughts, and your words, His words, and to ask God to close your mouth when you are not supposed to speak. When I ask God to close my mouth, I find that what I am about to say is prevented. In our own strength, we always seem to mess up, but if we ask God to intervene, the outcome is always better.

My dear brothers, take note of this: Everyone should be quick to listen, slow to speak and slow to become angry, for man's anger does not bring about the righteous life that God desires. James 1:19–20

We must make sure that our "yes" means yes and our "no" means no. In other words, keep our promises and commitments. Lying is not permissible; we are told in the book of Revelation that liars are thrown into the fiery pit. That's enough to convict us. The Bible instructs us to make a habit of never letting the sun go down on our anger. If we practice giving our anger up by sundown, the enemy will not be able to take a foothold in these dark areas. All these commands are a very tall order if we do not have Jesus. We can never change our stripes on our own, but if we focus on the stripes that Jesus took for us, we do it out of love.

But above all, my brethren, do not swear, either by heaven or by earth or with any other oath. But let your "Yes" be "Yes," and your "No," "No," lest you fall into judgment. James 5:12 (NKJV)

[Jesus said] "But I say to you that for every idle word men may speak, they will give account of it in the day of judgment. For by your words you will be justified, and by your words you will be condemned." Matthew 12:36–37 (NKJV)

But now you must rid yourselves of all such things as these: anger, rage, malice, slander, and filthy language from your lips. Do not lie to each other, since you have taken off your old self with its practices and have put on the new self, which is being renewed in knowledge in the image of its Creator. Colossians 3:8–10

"…But the cowardly, the unbelieving, the vile, the murderers, the sexually immoral, those who practice magic arts, the idolaters and all liars—their place will be in the fiery lake of burning sulfur. This is the second death." Revelation 21:8

…To put off your old self, which belongs to your former manner of life and is corrupt through deceitful desires, and to be renewed in the spirit of your minds, and to put on the new self, created after the likeness of God in true righteousness and holiness. Therefore, having put away falsehood, let each one of you speak the truth with his neighbor, for we are members one of another. Be angry and do not sin; do not let the sun go down on your anger, and give no opportunity to the devil. Ephesians 4:22–27 (ESV)

Finally, we must glorify the Lord in our actions. We glorify Him when we are joyful and thankful that Jesus has washed away our sins and we are pure as snow. We glorify Him when friends and family want to be around us because we are naturally positive and uplifting as well as when we walk beside someone and share their pain. We glorify Him when we do not show favoritism and treat everyone as better than ourselves. We glorify God when we are obedient servants to His wishes. The very best way to glorify the Lord with our actions is to let the light of Jesus shine through us. Pray that Jesus gives you His eyes to see people and His love to work through you. If only we can get out of our own way and humble ourselves to the point of a gentle, joyous bond servant. We can all take hope that God promises to work on us until the day that Jesus returns.

If you really keep the royal law found in Scripture, "Love your neighbor as yourself," you are doing right. But if you show favoritism, you sin and are convicted by the law as lawbreakers. James 2:8–9

Do nothing from selfishness or empty conceit, but with humility of mind let each of you regard one another as more important than himself; do not merely look out for your own personal interests, but also for the interests of others. Have this attitude in yourselves which was also in Christ Jesus, who, although He existed in the form of God, did not regard equality with God a thing to be grasped, but emptied Himself, taking the form of a bond-servant, and being made in the likeness of men. Being found in appearance as a man, He humbled Himself by becoming obedient to the point of death, even death on a cross. Philippians 2:3–8 (NASB)

In the same way, let your light shine before others, so that they may see your good works and give glory to your Father who is in heaven. Matthew 5:16 (ESV)

And whatever you do in word or deed, do all in the name of the Lord Jesus, giving thanks to God the Father through Him. Colossians 3:17 (NKJV)

Journaling Exercise

1. Please listen online to "God With Us" by MercyMe. Lift up your arms and the name of Jesus and glorify Him. As the song says, it is "such a tiny offering compared to Calvary."
2. In this lesson is there anything that you have been convicted to change?

WEEK 5
GROUP QUESTIONS

1. Explain what the Abrahamic Covenant is.

2. What has been harder for you in your walk of faith: receiving the knowledge of what Jesus did for you, believing that what He did on the cross was enough, or trusting that God is in control?

3. Share trials in your life where your faith was tested.

4. Share your experience of being baptized.

5. If you haven't been baptized out of obedience with full knowledge that you want to die to yourself and live for Jesus, share why. Pray together as a group to see if it is your time to be washed in the water.

6. What behavior in your life do you need to change so that you will glorify the Lord more? Pray for one another. The Bible says to confess your sins, pray for one another, and be healed.

Week 6

SUBMIT TO GOD

Blessed are they who keep his statutes and seek him with all their heart.
Psalm 119:2

Lesson 20

OBEDIENCE

As followers of Christ, we must be obedient to God's words. We have to show by our actions, not just our words or attending church, that we are following God's commandments and that we are being obedient to His will, like a humble servant, because we love Him. On the Day of Judgment, Jesus will look at our hearts. By grace we are saved, but our transformation and our work for the Kingdom that God has prepared for us will have their just rewards.

Heavenly Father, I pray that You will speak to me through Your Word and provide divine understanding of Your truth. Give me ears to hear and eyes to see and a heart to understand. In Jesus' name I pray, amen.

For we will all stand before God's judgment seat. It is written: "As surely as I live, says the Lord, 'every knee will bow before me; every tongue will confess to God.'" So then, each of us will give an account of himself to God. *Romans 14:10b–12*

So we make it our goal to please him, whether we are at home in the body or away from it. For we must all appear before the judgment seat of Christ, that each one may receive what is due him for all things done while in the body, whether good or bad. *2 Corinthians 5:9–10*

[Jesus said] "But I tell you that men will have to give account on the day of judgment for every careless word they have spoken. For

by your words you will be acquitted, and by your words you will be condemned." Matthew 12:36–37

[Jesus said] Not everyone who says to me, 'Lord, Lord,' will enter the kingdom of heaven, but only he who does the will of my Father who is in heaven. Many will say to me on that day, 'Lord, Lord, did we not prophesy in your name, and in your name drive out demons and perform many miracles?' Then I will tell them plainly, 'I never knew you. Away from me, you evildoers!' Matthew 7:21–23

By the grace God has given me, I laid a foundation as an expert builder, and someone else is building on it. But each one should be careful how he builds. For no one can lay any foundation other than the one already laid, which is Jesus Christ. If any man builds on this foundation, using gold, silver, costly stones, wood, hay or straw, his work will be shown for what it is because the Day will bring it to light. It will be revealed with fire, and the fire will test the quality of each man's work. If what he has built survives, he will receive his reward. If it is burned up, he will suffer loss; he himself will be saved, but only as one escaping through the flames. 1 Corinthians 3:10–15

What does the obedient Christian walk look like? We are to keep the Ten Commandments in Deuteronomy 5, and in addition to these, the Sermon on the Mount in Matthew 5, 6, & 7, which give us further instruction on Christian behavior. Take the time to read over these instructions. He did not come to abolish the Law, but to fulfill it. It is fulfilled for us by His love and His righteousness. His righteousness transfers to us when we accept Him into our lives and it allows us to grow more like Him. Our righteousness is never enough; so thank goodness we have a Savior whose righteousness is enough. We rejoice in this! If we truly know Him, we will delight in keeping His commands because they give us freedom. His burden is light and His yoke is easy. If we truly love Him, we will obey His commands. Remember, His greatest command is for us to love our God and one another.

By this we know that we have come to know Him, if we keep His commandments. The one who says, "I have come to know Him," and does not keep His commandments, is a liar, and the truth is not in him; but whoever keeps His word, in him the love of God has truly been perfected. By this we know that we are in Him: the one who says he abides in Him ought himself to walk in the same manner as He walked. 1 John 2:3–6 (NASB)

Whoever believes that Jesus is the Christ is born of God; and whoever loves the Father loves the child born of Him. By this we know that we love the children of God, when we love God and observe His commandments. For this is the love of God, that we keep His commandments; and His commandments are not burdensome. For whatever is born of God overcomes the world; and this is the victory that has overcome the world—our faith. 1 John 5:1–4 (NASB)

As the Father loved Me, I also have loved you; abide in My love. If you keep My commandments, you will abide in My love, just as I have kept My Father's commandments and abide in His love. "These things I have spoken to you, that My joy may remain in you, and that your joy may be full. This is My commandment, that you love one another as I have loved you." John 15:9–12 (NKJV)

"Do not think that I came to destroy the Law or the Prophets. I did not come to destroy but to fulfill. For assuredly, I say to you, till heaven and earth pass away, one jot or one tittle will by no means pass from the law till all is fulfilled. Whoever therefore breaks one of the least of these commandments, and teaches men so, shall be called least in the kingdom of heaven; but whoever does and teaches them, he shall be called great in the kingdom of heaven." Matthew 5:17–19 (NKJV)

Live as free men, but do not use your freedom as a cover-up for evil; live as servants of God. Show proper respect to everyone. Love the brotherhood of believers, fear God, honor the king. 1 Peter 2:16–17

[Jesus said] "You, my brothers, were called to be free. But do not use your freedom to indulge the sinful nature, rather, serve one another

in love. The entire law is summed up in a single command: "Love your neighbor as yourself." Galatians 5:13–14

How do we make sure that Jesus knows us when we meet Him face to face? Peter instructs us how to make our election assured.

His divine power has granted to us all things that pertain to life and godliness, through the knowledge of him who called us to his own glory and excellence, by which he has granted to us his precious and very great promises, so that through them you may become partakers of the divine nature, having escaped from the corruption that is in the world because of sinful desire. For this very reason, make every effort to supplement your faith with virtue, and virtue with knowledge, and knowledge with self-control, and self-control with steadfastness, and steadfastness with godliness, and godliness with brotherly affection, and brotherly affection with love. For if these qualities are yours and are increasing, they keep you from being ineffective or unfruitful in the knowledge of our Lord Jesus Christ. For whoever lacks these qualities is so nearsighted that he is blind, having forgotten that he was cleansed from his former sins. Therefore, brothers, be all the more diligent to confirm your calling and election, for if you practice these qualities you will never fall. For in this way there will be richly provided for you an entrance into the eternal kingdom of our Lord and Savior Jesus Christ. 2 Peter 1:3–11 (ESV)

Therefore, preparing your minds for action, and being sober-minded, set your hope fully on the grace that will be brought to you at the revelation of Jesus Christ. As obedient children, do not be conformed to the passions of your former ignorance, but as he who called you is holy, you also be holy in all your conduct, since it is written, "You shall be holy, for I am holy." 1 Peter 1:13–16 (ESV)

Journaling Exercise

1. Ask Jesus to help you obey His commands. If we love Him, we will obey Him.

2. What do you need to work on in your actions?

The LORD redeems the life of his servants;
none of those who take refuge in him will be condemned.
Psalm 34:22 (ESV)

Lesson 21

CONDEMNATION

*G*et rid of any guilt or the voice of condemnation. (The definition of condemnation according to Webster's dictionary is: a statement or expression of very strong and definite criticism or disapproval.) The devil's main arsenal against us is condemnation. He brings forth this spirit of condemnation within us, which we in turn redirect as feeling unworthy, inferior, guilty, bitter, or rebellious. Even seemingly trivial things can be used by the devil to condemn us. You must rebuke these feelings by claiming, "There is no condemnation for those that are in Christ Jesus." Practice while praying out loud to visually **loose** the stronghold placed on you by the devil, and to **bind** your mind to the obedience of Jesus Christ, and His love. We must also examine the true deep sources of this condemnation and ask that these hurts, or strongholds, placed on us by the devil be healed by Jesus and taken away. Place them at the foot of the cross. You can ask Jesus to place His yoke upon you; for it is light, and His burdens are few. Any residual fears can be removed this way as well. His blood washes away our sins and by His stripes, we are healed. Understanding this is crucial to becoming more Christ-like in our behavior. Not only is He willing to forgive our sins, but He deeply desires to graciously remove them from our hearts.

Heavenly Father, I pray that You will speak to me through Your Word and provide divine understanding of Your truth. Give me ears to hear and eyes to see and a heart to understand. In Jesus' name I pray, amen.

Therefore, there is now no condemnation for those who are in Christ Jesus, because through Christ Jesus the law of the Spirit of life set me free from the law of sin and death. Romans 8:1

[Jesus said] For God did not send His Son into the world to condemn the world, but that the world through Him might be saved. "He who believes in Him is not condemned." John 3:17–18a (NKJV)

The weapons we fight with are not the weapons of the world. On the contrary, they have divine power to demolish strongholds. We demolish arguments and every pretension that sets itself up against the knowledge of God, and we take captive every thought to the obedience to Christ. 2 Corinthians 10:4–5

Yet the LORD longs to be gracious to you; he rises to show you compassion. For the LORD is a God of justice. Blessed are all who wait for him! Isaiah 30:18

But if we walk in the light as He is in the light, we have fellowship with one another, and the blood of Jesus Christ His Son cleanses us from all sin. 1 John 1:7 (NKJV)

And ought not this woman, being a daughter of Abraham, whom Satan hath bound, lo, these eighteen years, be loosed from this bond on the Sabbath day? Luke 13:16 (KJV)

"Assuredly, I say to you, whatever you bind on earth will be bound in heaven, and whatever you loose on earth will be loosed in heaven." Matthew 18:18 (NKJV)

We must be able to determine the difference between condemnation and conviction. When we feel guilty, helpless, or unworthy in our thoughts over a certain action, it is the devil condemning us of our faults. God does not torment us. He convicts us and follows it up with a solution to resolve it. If you feel an overwhelming sense of doubt, fear, or depression, resist the enemy by rebuking him and submitting yourself to God.

Submit yourselves, then, to God. Resist the devil and he will flee from you. James 4:7

Prayer Against Condemnation

*Heavenly Father, I declare in the name of Jesus that my righteous standing comes from Jesus Christ. As He is, which is at the right hand of God and full of righteousness, so am I in this world. Thank you LORD for giving me Your Spirit within me that is greater than he who is in the world. It is written, "For you did not receive a spirit that makes you a slave again to fear, but you received the Spirit of sonship." I claim my inheritance as a son/daughter of God that sits at Your table and I am a co-heir with Christ, **so get behind me, Satan**.*

There is no condemnation for those that are in Christ Jesus. I loose any power the devil has over my mind and I bind my mind to the obedience of Jesus Christ. As it is written, whatever is loosed on earth is loosed in heaven, and whatever is bound on earth is bound in heaven.

I can do all things through Christ who strengthens me. I plead the blood of Jesus over me and ask for the peace of God, a peace that surpasses all understanding and guards my heart and mind in Christ Jesus. I surrender all to You, Jesus. In Your Holy Name I pray, amen.

Journaling Exercise

1. What is the devil trying to use to condemn you?

2. What issues do you need to put at the foot of the cross and ask Jesus to remove from you?

3. Please listen online to "I Surrender All" and feel the peace that comes from singing this hymn.

You shall eat the fruit of the labor of your hands;
you shall be blessed, and it shall be well with you.
Psalm 128:2 (ESV)

Lesson 22
OPEN THE FLOODGATES

*T*he only place in the Bible that God says to test Him to see that in return He will "open the floodgates of Heaven and pours out so much blessing" is in regard to tithing. He requires that we give the first fruits (10%) that we earn to His Kingdom, His storehouse, which is the church that you attend. Anything beyond that is considered generous, blessed giving. We are the descendants of Abraham and Jacob because we, Gentiles, are grafted into the olive tree by our faith. All that we have comes from God, so we must give with a gracious, loving heart, or it will all be for nothing. God wants us to trust Him in all things, and tithing demonstrates that we are trusting and obeying Him. Remember that where your treasure is, so will your heart be also.

Heavenly Father, I pray that You speak to me through Your Word and provide divine understanding of Your truth. Give me ears to hear and eyes to see and a heart to understand. In Jesus' name I pray, amen.

"I the LORD do not change. So you, O descendants of Jacob, are not destroyed. Ever since the time of your forefathers you have turned away from my decrees and have not kept them. Return to me, and I will return to you," says the LORD Almighty. "But you ask, 'How are we to return?'—"Will a man rob God? Yet you rob me. "But you ask, 'How do we rob you?' "In tithes and offerings. You are under a curse—the whole nation of you—because you are robbing me. Bring the whole

tithe into the storehouse, that there may be food in my house. Test me in this," says the Lord Almighty, "and see if I will not throw open the floodgates of heaven and pour out so much blessing that you will not have room for it." Malachi 3:6–10

Honor the LORD with your wealth, with the first fruits of all your crops, then your barns will be filled to overflowing, and your vats will brim over with new wine. Proverbs 3:9

[Jesus said] "Woe to you, scribes and Pharisees, hypocrites! For you tithe mint and dill and cummin, and have neglected the weightier provisions of the law: justice and mercy and faithfulness; but these are the things you should have done without neglecting the others." Matthew 23:23 (NASB)

Now this I say, he who sows sparingly will also reap sparingly, and he who sows bountifully will also reap bountifully. Each one must do just as he has purposed in his heart, not grudgingly or under compulsion, for God loves a cheerful giver. 2 Corinthians 9:6–7 (NASB)

And He sat down opposite the treasury, and began observing how the people were putting money into the treasury; and many rich people were putting in large sums. A poor widow came and put in two small copper coins, which amount to a cent. Calling His disciples to Him, He said to them, "Truly I say to you, this poor widow put in more than all the contributors to the treasury; for they all put in out of their surplus, but she, out of her poverty, put in all she owned, all she had to live on." Mark 12:41–44 (NASB)

[Jesus said] "Give, and it will be given to you. A good measure, pressed down, shaken together and running over, will be poured into your lap. For with the measure you use, it will be measured to you." Luke 6:38

For the love of money is a root of all kinds of evil. Some people, eager for money, have wandered from the faith and pierced themselves with many griefs. 1 Timothy 6:10

"No one can serve two masters, for either he will hate the one and love the other, or he will be devoted to the one and despise the other. You cannot serve God and money." Matthew 6:24 (ESV)

[Jesus said] "Do not lay up for yourselves treasures on earth, where moth and rust destroy and where thieves break in and steal, but lay up for yourselves treasures in heaven, where neither moth nor rust destroys and where thieves do not break in and steal. For where your treasure is, there your heart will be also." Matthew 6:19–21 (ESV)

"Beware of practicing your righteousness before other people in order to be seen by them, for then you will have no reward from your Father who is in heaven. "Thus, when you give to the needy, sound no trumpet before you, as the hypocrites do in the synagogues and in the streets, that they may be praised by others. Truly, I say to you, they have received their reward. But when you give to the needy, do not let your left hand know what your right hand is doing, so that your giving may be in secret. And your Father who sees in secret will reward you." Matthew 6:1–4 (ESV)

If I give away all I have, and if I deliver up my body to be burned, but have not love, I gain nothing. 1 Corinthians 13:3 (ESV)

Journaling Exercise

1. Write down the blessings bestowed upon you when you tithe.

2. If you have never fully tithed, do so and journal what transpired from your act of obedience. It is truly a joy to fully trust God in your finances.

They asked, and he brought quail,
and gave them bread from heaven in abundance.
Psalm 105:40 (ESV)

Lesson 23
THE BREAD OF LIFE

*J*esus is the bread of life that we need daily. He *is* the manna from heaven that was sent down to give us life. In John 6:35 (ESV), Jesus said to them, "I am the bread of life; whoever comes to me shall not hunger, and whoever believes in me shall never thirst." He came down to reconcile us and give us eternal life.

It is important to take communion on a regular basis to remember what He did for us on the cross and to be reminded of the forgiveness of our sins. As you take the bread, do so in honor of His body that was broken for you to be healed and the wine is His blood that He shed so that you are *forgiven of all sins.* There is no guilt, only gratitude. This is a blood covenant relationship that Jesus made so that our sins are forgiven through His sacrifice. The bread and wine are an important part of Jesus making this covenant and for us to remember it. A covenant is a solemn binding agreement. We have peace of mind knowing that we are in a covenant relationship with our Sovereign LORD that He will not break.

Heavenly Father, I pray that You will speak to me through Your Word and provide divine understanding of Your truth. Give me ears to hear and eyes to see and a heart to understand. In Jesus' name I pray, amen.

While they were eating, Jesus took some bread, and after a blessing, He broke it and gave it to the disciples, and said, "Take, eat; this is My body." And when He had taken a cup and given thanks, He gave

it to them, saying, "Drink from it, all of you; for this is My blood of the covenant, which is poured out for many for forgiveness of sins." Matthew 26:26–28 (NASB)

So Jesus said to them, "Truly, truly, I say to you, unless you eat the flesh of the Son of Man and drink His blood, you have no life in yourselves. He who eats My flesh and drinks My blood has eternal life, and I will raise him up on the last day. For My flesh is true food, and My blood is true drink. He who eats My flesh and drinks My blood abides in Me, and I in him. As the living Father sent Me, and I live because of the Father, so he who eats Me, he also will live because of Me. This is the bread which came down out of heaven; not as the fathers ate and died; he who eats this bread will live forever." John 6:53–58 (NASB)

When taking communion, we are called to examine our hearts and ask for forgiveness of any known sins. This is between you and Jesus as you alone will stand before Him on the Day of Judgment. If you read all the verses in 1 Corinthians 11, Paul adamantly tells us that every time we take communion or when we eat and drink together with believers, we must recognize the body of Christ, in order that we do not have judgment on ourselves. Before eating as the family of Christ, Paul instructs us to wait for everyone to sit down and to give thanks and recognition to Jesus and ask that this food be blessed to our bodies.

When you come together, it is not the Lord's Supper you eat, for as you eat, each of you goes ahead without waiting for anybody else. One remains hungry, another gets drunk. Don't you have homes to eat and drink in? Or do you despise the church of God and humiliate those who have nothing? What shall I say to you? Shall I praise you for this? Certainly not! 1 Corinthians 11:20–22

Therefore whoever eats the bread or drinks the cup of the Lord in an unworthy manner, shall be guilty of the body and the blood of the Lord. But a man must examine himself, and in so doing he is to eat of the bread and drink of the cup. For he who eats and drinks, eats and drinks judgment to himself if he does not judge the body rightly. For this reason many among you are weak and sick, and a number sleep. But if we judged ourselves rightly, we would not be judged. But when we are judged, we are disciplined by the Lord so that we will not be condemned along with the world. 1 Corinthians 11:27–32 (NASB)

Now the Spirit expressly says that in latter times some will depart from the faith, giving heed to deceiving spirits and doctrines of demons, speaking lies in hypocrisy, having their own conscience seared with a hot iron, forbidding to marry, and commanding to abstain from foods which God created to be received with thanksgiving by those who believe and know the truth. For every creature of God is good, and nothing is to be refused if it is received with thanksgiving; for it is sanctified by the word of God and prayer. 1 Timothy 4:1–5 (NKJV)

While you are taking communion, or giving the blessing over a gathered meal, remember that this is a precursor to the meal to come when we are invited to the wedding supper of the Lamb. Acknowledge this day in your prayer. We rejoice and look forward in anticipation to the feast with Jesus!

Then I heard what seemed to be the voice of a great multitude, like the roar of many waters and like the sound of mighty peals of thunder, crying out, "Hallelujah! For the Lord our God the Almighty reigns. Let us rejoice and exult and give him the glory, for the marriage of the Lamb has come, and his Bride has made herself ready; it was granted her to clothe herself with fine linen, bright and pure"— for the fine linen is the righteous deeds of the saints. And the angel said to me, "Write this: Blessed are those who are invited to the marriage supper of the Lamb." And he said to me, "These are the true words of God." Revelation 19:6–9 (ESV)

Journaling Exercise

1. Give examples of blessed times when you came together in a meal and thanked Jesus. If you have never done it, invite someone over and pray

before you eat together. To ensure that the meal is blessed, when you start to prepare it ask God to bless it and help you make it good.

WEEK 6
GROUP QUESTIONS

1. List the 10 Commandments in order. (Deuteronomy 5)

2. List The Beatitudes of who is blessed. (Matthew 5:1–12)

3. Are we exempt from the Law now that we are under Grace? (Matthew 5:18–19)

4. What is the devil trying to condemn you with? Pray for one another and use the Prayer for Condemnation.

5. What did you learn about tithing? Does anyone have an example where God rewarded you for your obedience to tithe?

6. Why is receiving communion so important?

7. Look over next week's lesson on fasting and breaking strongholds. Determine a day that would work well to fast as a group or with your buddy.

Week 7

SEEKING GOD'S WILL

Wait on the LORD: be of good courage, and he shall strengthen thine heart: wait, I say, on the LORD.
Psalm 27:14 (KJV)

Lesson 24
LET YOUR REQUESTS BE KNOWN

Relinquish your will to God; follow His prodding. In His perfect timing, God will make everything that is His will happen in your life. We must pray effectively and often to God to receive what He so freely wants to give. God knows our heart and desires and we must ask in order to receive. Go to your prayer closet and let your requests be known to Him. Ask for spiritual wisdom and understanding of His will. His will, not yours. God wants us to seek solitude and listen in the silence. It is in the quiet that He teaches. God instructs us to "Be still, and know that I am God." (Psalm 46:10a) You will find that we will have periods of solitude in our lives. He uses them to help us grow.

Heavenly Father, I pray that You will speak to me through Your Word and provide divine understanding of Your truth. Give me ears to hear and eyes to see and a heart to understand. In Jesus' name I pray, amen.

For this reason, since the day we heard about you, we have not stopped praying for you and asking God to fill you with the knowledge of his will through all spiritual wisdom and understanding. *Colossians 1:9*

If any of you lacks wisdom, he should ask God, who gives generously to all without finding fault, and it will be given to him. But when he asks, he must believe and not doubt, because he who doubts is like a wave of the sea, blown and tossed by the wind. *James 1:5–6*

Trust in the LORD with all your heart, and lean not on your own understanding; in all your ways acknowledge him, and he will make your paths straight. Proverbs 3:5–6

Now this is the confidence that we have in Him, that if we ask anything according to His will, He hears us. And if we know that He hears us, whatever we ask, we know that we have the petitions that we have asked of Him. 1 John 5:14–15 (NKJV)

[Jesus said] "But when you pray, go into your room, close the door and pray to your Father, who is unseen. Then your Father who sees what is done in secret, will reward you." Matthew 6:6

Be still, and know that I am God; I will be exalted among the nations, I will be exalted in the earth! The LORD of hosts is with us; the God of Jacob is our refuge. Selah. Psalm 46:10–11 (NKJV)

We are better able to receive guidance when we know that Jesus <u>always</u> loves us deeply and would have given His life if only for you. This gratitude opens the communication of the Holy Spirit within us. We must be so thankful for this love and give deep reverence to God with our words of praise and thanksgiving. Ask God for an utterance, a word, from the Holy Spirit. I have asked Him "yes, no, or wait?" Listen for an answer. If you feel that God has turned His hearing from you, ask Him to search your heart and if there are any offensive ways to reveal them so that you can repent.

Once you believe you have been answered by God, ask it again to confirm His message. When God told David to fight the Philistines, his men were afraid, so he asked God again and was told again that he would be victorious. What you are supposed to learn will become apparent if you seek Him with all your heart.

[Jesus said] And I will ask the Father, and he will give you another Counselor to be with you forever, the Spirit of truth. John 14:16–17a

Withal praying also for us, that God would open unto us a door of utterance, to speak the mystery of Christ, for which I am also in bonds. Colossians 4:3 (KJV)

The effectual fervent prayer of a righteous man availeth much. James 5:16b (KJV)

Search me, O God, and know my heart; test me and know my anxious thoughts. See if there is any offensive way in me, and lead me in the way everlasting. Psalm 139:23–24

Rejoice evermore. Pray without ceasing. 1 Thessalonians 5:16–17a

Sometimes the answer from God is "wait." When asking for direction from God, plead your case and then wait in faith with a quiet patience. Be strong and keep reminding yourself that you only want God's will for your life. A peace will come when you know that you are waiting on the LORD.

Journaling Exercise

1. Please listen online to "Overwhelmed" by Big Daddy. Delight in the greatness of God.
2. Go to where you like to spend time with God and let your requests be known to Him.

3. Write down how He answers you.

Send out your light and your truth; let them lead me;
let them bring me to your holy hill and to your dwelling!
Psalm 43:3 (ESV)

Lesson 25

REVELATION

God's word, our Bible, will always be the truth of His will. We must pray without ceasing and stay in His word every day, not just when we want an answer. Reading our Bible is how we stay obedient to God, learn what we need to hear from Him, and it keeps our sinful nature at bay. God calls us to go even deeper in our relationship with Him.

It is the Holy Spirit within us that draws us out of the natural world and into the realm of the supernatural where God can reveal to us an infinite dimension. By humbly submitting and opening yourself up to His Spirit, God can give you revelation. Seek His Face as you pray for spiritual wisdom and revelation. Spend quiet time with Him. Know that in our flesh we do not have the answers but He has them all. It is hard to understand this in the natural world; but God is omnipresent, omnipotent, and omniscient. This means that He is always present, all-powerful, and all knowing.

God's Spirit dwells with us to communicate with us. He can communicate with us however He chooses; He is the Lord God Almighty. Though we have nothing to give to God that He would ever need, He continues to love and help us. He created us and owns us. God is always working for our good, even if it doesn't seem that way at the time. The scriptures tell us that "Our God is in heaven; he does whatever pleases him." (Psalm 115:3)

Events in our life happen for a reason. As humans, we will never fully comprehend why God allow things to happen. We can go to Him with our discontent but that doesn't mean we will ever know His reasons. We must always keep in mind that God is in control. He is the Creator of the Universe. Where were we to give advice when He created the world? We see things from a very small view while His view is infinite and based on the eternal. His ways are higher than our ways, His thoughts higher than our thoughts. If we try to go it alone, we will inevitably make a mess of it. I've been there, done that. How about you? Trust that He always knows best and seek to have Him reveal His will for you.

I have a testimony on how God used dreams and fasting to give me revelation. Just to set the stage, before I was a Christian, God gave me a dream where I remembered every vivid detail of the scene that I was in and He gave me this same dream for three nights. In my dream I was standing in a circle having a discussion with construction workers and we were all in yellow hard hats. I was the only woman in the circle. The difference was that my belly was protruding as I spoke to them because I was quite far along in my pregnancy. Five years later I stood in this very circle, with the construction workers, all in yellow hard hats, pregnant with my daughter, and I was living that dream. I realized that God can speak through dreams.

When my daughter was two years old, I had three nights of a very vivid dream of me walking along a forested path with my two children running ahead of me and crossing over a small foot bridge. My husband and I were having a discussion about him taking a job in Ohio and I knew that this was where the forest was located. God had also told me in the dream that we would be there for five years. We went to Ohio where it was not easy to leave our extended family. We entered into a desert time where our small family felt quite alone. God used this time to draw us near to Him. At the cul-du-sac of our street was a path through the forest. The dream became reality as my children ran down the tree-lined path in front of me over that same foot bridge. To the month, we were in Ohio for five years.

God then brought us to the state of Washington with the same company. For two and a half years we tried to sell our house in Ohio. The first year we had it on the market for five months until we had no money left and God brought a renter in our final hour. We tried again the following spring, but no buyer. The third spring we came to Ohio to try again. We painted all the interior walls and had the bathroom remodeled. This time everything fell into place to get things done and God's hand was on it in a mighty way. It sold the second day on the market.

My husband became upset about how much money we had lost from purchasing this home at the top of the market and all the money we had put in upkeep and updating to sell. God called me to fast and pray about this house and ask for a revelation. This is what the Holy Spirit revealed to me as I cried and received it: "What you lost is nothing to what you gained." Wow! What did we gain from this house? I found Jesus in Ohio. My husband came back to Jesus in Ohio. Our marriage was saved in Ohio. Can eternity with Jesus and a saved marriage compare one bit to losing money? That was a revelation!

Heavenly Father, I pray that You will speak to me through Your Word and provide divine understanding of Your truth. Give me ears to hear and eyes to see and a heart to understand. In Jesus' name I pray, amen.

The LORD does whatever pleases him, in the heavens and on the earth, in the seas and all their depths. *Psalm 135:6*

He who forms the mountains, creates the wind, and reveals his thoughts to man, he who turns dawn to darkness, and treads the high places of the earth—the LORD God Almighty is his name. *Amos 4:13*

Where were you when I laid the earth's foundation? Tell me, if you understand. *Job 38:4*

Woe to him who quarrels with his Maker, to him who is but a potsherd among the potsherds on the ground. Does the clay say to the potter, 'What are you making?' Does the work say, 'He has no hands.'? *Isaiah 45:9*

"Is it by your understanding that the hawk soars and spreads his wings toward the south? Is it at your command that the eagle mounts up and makes his nest on high? On the rock he dwells and makes his home, on the rocky crag and stronghold. From there he spies out the prey; his eyes behold it from far away. His young ones suck up blood, and where the slain are, there is he. And the LORD said to Job: "Shall a faultfinder contend with the Almighty? He who argues with God, let him answer it." *Job 39:26–30 & Job 40:1–2 (ESV)*

As the heavens are higher than the earth, so are my ways higher than your ways and my thoughts than your thoughts. Isaiah 55:9

The older and wiser we get, the more we <u>know</u> that we know nothing. The Bible tells us that blessed are the poor in spirit, those who realize they are nothing and can do nothing without God. He alone is in control. A song by J.J. Heller has a great verse that says to God: "I don't know what you're doing, but I know who you are." Trust that He knows best and praise His Holy Name. Increase your faith by pondering on His love and greatness and that He sits on the throne. Look back at how He has always seen you through in the past.

There are a few things that we can hold onto: How awesome is it that God cares so much for us that He gave us a way back to Him through the death of His Son, seeks us out over and over, draws us near, teaches us His ways, desires for us to be prosperous, and wants us to dwell with Him for eternity?

"…Naked I came from my mother's womb, and naked I will depart, The LORD gave and the LORD has taken away, may the name of the LORD be praised." Job 1:21

When I first started seeking to hear from God, a small book was given to me entitled, "Come Away My Beloved" by Frances J. Roberts, 1973. God really spoke to me through this anointed book of how much He loved me. I would pray for a word from Him and open up this book and it poured out. I have prayed for others with this book and it spoke to them as well. It is a keepsake that is still available. One of my favorite lines in the book is "He seeth Me most clearly who lovest Me most dearly."

When seeking to hear from God, pray for spiritual wisdom and revelation of His truth and open up your Bible. Be open to any way that God communicates with you because He can do it however He pleases. God will reveal Himself to you in a personal way. Ask, seek, knock, and the door will be opened.

For thus says the LORD, who created the heavens, who is God, who formed the earth and made it, who has established it, who did not create it in vain, who formed it to be inhabited: "I am the LORD, and there is no other. I have not spoken in secret, in a dark place of the earth; I did not say to the seed of Jacob, 'Seek Me in vain'; I, the LORD, speak righteousness, I declare things that are right. Isaiah 45:18–19 (NKJV)

[Jesus said] "Ask and it will be given to you; seek and you will find; knock and the door will be opened to you. For everyone who asks receives; he who seeks finds; and to him who knocks, the door will be opened." Matthew 7:7–8

God has a path for all of us, the right path, the good way, the path of righteousness. If we seek to hear Him with all our heart and all our soul, He will reveal this path.

The LORD is my shepherd, I shall not be in want. He makes me lie down in green pastures, he leads me beside quiet waters, he restores my soul. He guides me in paths of righteousness for his name's sake. Psalm 23:1–3

Make me to know your ways, O LORD; teach me your paths. Lead me in your truth and teach me, for you are the God of my salvation; for you I wait all the day long. Psalm 25:4–5 (ESV)

Hear, O LORD, when I cry with my voice! Have mercy also upon me, and answer me. When You said, "Seek My face," My heart said to You, "Your face, LORD, I will seek." Psalm 27:7–8 (NKJV)

Whether you turn to the right or to the left, your ears will hear a voice behind you, saying, "This is the way; walk in it." Isaiah 30:21

This is what the LORD says: "Stand at the crossroads and look; ask for the ancient paths, ask where the good way is, and walk in it, and you will find rest for your souls." Jeremiah 6:16a

Example of a Prayer for Revelation

Heavenly Father, Creator of the heavens and the earth, Maker of us all, I praise Your Almighty Name. You parted the sea. You command the eagle to fly. You are the source of

all wisdom. Your ways are higher than mine and Your thoughts are higher than mine and I seek to know Your will, LORD, not mine. I ask that You give me spiritual wisdom and revelation to hear Your will. Holy Spirit, please be present in me and speak to me.

Abba, I cry out to you. I seek your face, O LORD. I want to know You more. I want to feel You more. You knew me before I was even born and I want whatever Your plan is for my life. I love you LORD and thank you that You first loved me. In Jeremiah 6:16, You say to "stand at the crossroads and look; ask for the ancient paths, ask where the good way is and walk in it, and you will find rest for your souls."

LORD, I need revelation of _____. I ask that You show me the ancient paths and where the good way is. I desire Your path of righteousness.

In Jesus' precious name I pray, amen.

Journaling Exercise

1. Please listen online to the song "King of the World" by Natalie Grant and then to "I Surrender" by Hillsong Live.
2. After asking God for His wisdom and revelation, how and what did He reveal to you?

[Helpful hint if you lose or misplace something: Pray to God that "what is hidden let it be revealed." —It works every time. God is so gracious.]

Behold, You desire truth in the innermost being,
And in the hidden part You will make me know wisdom.
Psalm 51:6 (NASB)

Lesson 26

FASTING

One way to receive spiritual wisdom and revelation is to fast. Fasting breaks the bonds of wickedness and any authority we have allowed the devil to have in our life and also shows humility in our circumstances as we cry out to God. You will know when you are called to fast by the Lord. Fasting is under God's grace and His strength, and He will tell you if you need to fast longer than a day or less than a day. Fasting is not showing God how disciplined you are, but rather that you are wholeheartedly seeking His wisdom or deliverance. From sunrise to sunset drink only water and get down on your knees and pray earnestly. You can also fast with another believer and pray in agreement. Jesus says that where two or more are gathered in His name, He is there also. Notice that Jesus does not say "if" you fast but "when" you fast. God is so faithful to answer when you seek Him with all your heart.

Heavenly Father, I pray that You will speak to me through Your Word and provide divine understanding of Your truth. Give me ears to hear and eyes to see and a heart to understand. In Jesus' name I pray, Amen.

And Jesus rebuked him and the demon came out of him, and the boy was cured at once. Then the disciples came to Jesus privately, and said, "Why could we not drive it out?" And he said to them, "Because of the littleness of your faith; for truly I say to you, if you have faith as a mustard seed, you shall say to this mountain, "Move from

here to there,' and it shall move, and nothing shall be impossible to you. "But this kind does not go out except by prayer and fasting." Matthew 17:18–21 (NASB)

"And when you fast, do not look gloomy like the hypocrites, for they disfigure their faces that their fasting may be seen by others. Truly, I say to you, they have received their reward. But when you fast, anoint your head and wash your face, that your fasting may not be seen by others but by your Father who is in secret. And your Father who sees in secret will reward you." Matthew 6:16–18 (ESV)

'Why have we fasted, and you see it not? Why have we humbled ourselves, and you take no knowledge of it?' Behold, in the day of your fast you seek your own pleasure, and oppress all your workers. Behold, you fast only to quarrel and to fight and to hit with a wicked fist. Fasting like yours this day will not make your voice to be heard on high. Is such the fast that I choose, a day for a person to humble himself? Is it to bow down his head like a reed, and to spread sackcloth and ashes under him? Will you call this a fast, and a day acceptable to the LORD? "Is not this the fast that I choose: to loose the bonds of wickedness, to undo the straps of the yoke, to let the oppressed go free, and to break every yoke?" Isaiah 58:3–6 (ESV)

"Even now," declares the LORD, "return to me with all your heart, with fasting and weeping and mourning." Joel 2:12

Journaling Exercise

1. Read ahead to Lesson 27 and list issues that you need an answer or to be delivered from through prayer and fasting. Prayerfully consider fasting for the next lesson. If you have a Christian friend or family member that might fast with you, give them a call. If you are in a group, perhaps contact some of your members. It can be life-changing.

The LORD is my rock and my fortress and my deliverer, my God, my rock, in whom I take refuge, my shield, and the horn of my salvation, my stronghold.
Psalm 18:2 (ESV)

Lesson 27
BREAKING STRONGHOLDS

*T*he only stronghold in our life should be Jesus. Everything we do, say, and think should be directly connected to Him. Unfortunately, we all come with baggage and we need to deal with it. After removing these strongholds out of our life, we can then be effective servants of our Lord Jesus. The skeletons in our closet need His light to shine on them so they can come out of the dark, be verbally confessed, and removed from our hearts.

Our Bible tells us that the unbeliever who sins passes on curses to their third and fourth generation. The sins of our fathers are forgiven by the blood of Jesus when we believe in Him. Jesus redeemed us from the curse by becoming a curse for us as He suffered on the cross. Sometimes it is necessary to verbally confess the sins of our fathers to be released from the bondage that can still be present. Examples would include: the spirit of unbelief, fears passed down, making false idols, the spirit of infirmity, the spirit of confusion, the spirit of worldliness, the spirit of Jezebel, mental illness, a complaining heart, disobedience, self-righteousness, an evil tongue (wicked words/profanity), lying, a false witness, a heart that devises wicked schemes, hands that shed innocent blood, haughty eyes, feet that rush into evil, sexual immorality, sexual hang-ups, adultery, drunkenness, witchcraft/magical arts, and perhaps any of these sins: pride, envy, gluttony, lust, anger, greed, and sloth. Break these strongholds and curses by fasting and asking them to be removed from you and your future generations.

Heavenly Father, I pray that You will speak to me through Your Word and provide divine understanding of Your truth. Give me ears to hear and eyes to see and a heart to understand. In Jesus' name I pray, amen.

"You shall not make for yourself a carved image, or any likeness of anything that is in heaven above, or that is in the earth beneath, or that is in the water under the earth. You shall not bow down to them or serve them, for I the LORD your God am a jealous God, visiting the iniquity of the fathers on the children to the third and the fourth generation of those who hate me, but showing steadfast love to thousands of those who love me and keep my commandments." *Exodus 20:4–6 (ESV)*

Christ redeemed us from the curse of the law by becoming a curse for us, for it is written: "Cursed is everyone who is hung on a tree." He redeemed us in order that the blessing given to Abraham might come to the Gentiles through Christ Jesus, so that by faith we might receive the promise of the Spirit. *Galatians 3:13–14*

He brought them out of darkness and the deepest gloom and broke away their chains. *Psalm 107:14*

Prayer for Generational Cures and Strongholds

In the name of Jesus, I confess the sins and iniquities of my parents, (name specific sins), grandparents (list sins), all other ancestors (list sins) and my own sins (list). I ask to be released of any bondage brought about by generational curses passed down from my ancestors. If there is the bondage of pride, envy, gluttony, lust, anger, greed or sloth, in the name of the LORD, I cut them off. I renounce all unknown sins and unbelief from my ancestors. In Mark, verse 9:24, it is written, "I do believe; help me overcome my unbelief!" Help me, Jesus, to overcome any unbelief I may have. The LORD has said in the book of Isaiah, "Is not this the fast that I choose: to loose the bonds of wickedness, to undo the straps of the yoke, to let the oppressed go free, and to break every yoke?" I ask to break every yoke and any bonds of wickedness and oppression from my ancestors. Christ redeemed us from the curse of the law by dying for us and I declare that by the blood of Jesus, these sins have been forgiven and Satan and his demons can no longer use these sins as legal grounds in my life.

I ask forgiveness for acting in agreement with the curses and unbelief of my parents, grandparents, and ancestors. I forgive my ancestors for any sins passed down. In the name of Jesus Christ, and by the power of His blood, I now declare that all generational unbelief, strongholds, hexes, vexes, and curses have been renounced, broken and severed, and that I am no longer under their bondage. I give them all to you, Jesus.

In the name of Jesus, I declare myself and my future generations loosed from any bondage passed down to me from my ancestors and bound to the obedience of Jesus Christ. As you are, Jesus, at the right hand side of our Heavenly Father and full of righteousness, so am I on this earth. In Jesus' mighty name I pray, amen.

Listen online to "Break Every Chain" (Feat. Kim Walker). Every time you hear "break every chain," think of, and list, something you need to release and give to Jesus. In the future, if the enemy tries to come at you with what you listed as your strongholds and generational curses, deny any authority by saying, "I rebuke that. I am no longer under that curse. I have been delivered and set free by Jesus Christ, who is my authority."

Journaling Exercise
1. What did you learn after fasting?

2. Please listen online to "Flawless" by MercyMe. Give thanks that your family baggage is no longer yours because of the cross.

WEEK 7
GROUP QUESTIONS

1. What requests do you have for God? Lift them up in prayer.

2. Was anything revealed by God to you this week? How was it revealed?

3. What is the significance of fasting?

4. Were any strongholds in your life broken from fasting? Share your experience.

Week 8

THE HOLY SPIRIT

Teach me to do your will, for you are my God!
Let your good Spirit lead me on level ground!
Psalm 143:10 (ESV)

Lesson 28

FRUIT OF THE SPIRIT

*T*he fruit of the Holy Spirit consists of nine traits: love, joy, peace, patience, kindness, goodness, faithfulness, gentleness, and self-control. By dying to what bound us to our sinful nature through the death and resurrection of Jesus, we repent from our old ways of the flesh and are released to the new way of the Spirit. We will enjoy the fruit of the Spirit as we grow in Jesus.

Heavenly Father, I pray that You will speak to me through Your Word and provide divine understanding of Your truth. Give me ears to hear and eyes to see and a heart to understand. In Jesus' name I pray, amen.

> **But the fruit of the Spirit is love, joy, peace, patience, kindness, goodness, faithfulness, gentleness and self-control...** *Galatians 5:22–23*
>
> **For you were once darkness, but now you are light in the Lord. Walk as children of light (for the fruit of the Spirit is in all goodness, righteousness, and truth), finding out what is acceptable to the Lord. And have no fellowship with the unfruitful works of darkness, but rather expose them.** *Ephesians 5:8–11 (NKJV)*
>
> **And now these three remain: faith, hope and love. But the greatest of these is love.** *1 Corinthians 13:13*
>
> **Produce fruit in keeping with repentance.** *Matthew 3:8*
>
> **The mind of sinful man is death, but the mind controlled by the Spirit is life and peace.** *Romans 8:6*

How do we produce good fruit? The true vine is Jesus and we are the branches. We must remain, or abide, in Jesus to produce good fruit.

> *"I am the true vine, and My Father is the vinedresser. Every branch in Me that does not bear fruit He takes away; and every branch that bears fruit He prunes, that it may bear more fruit. You are already clean because of the word which I have spoken to you. Abide in Me, and I in you. As the branch cannot bear fruit of itself, unless it abides in the vine, neither can you, unless you abide in Me. "I am the vine, you are the branches. He who abides in Me, and I in him, bears much fruit; for without Me you can do nothing."* John 15:1–5 (NKJV)
>
> *Greater love has no one than this, than to lay down one's life for his friends. You are My friends if you do whatever I command you. No longer do I call you servants, for a servant does not know what his master is doing; but I have called you friends, for all things that I heard from My Father I have made known to you. You did not choose Me, but I chose you and appointed you that you should go and bear fruit, and that your fruit should remain, that whatever you ask the Father in My name He may give you. These things I command you, that you love one another.* John 15:13–17 (NKJV)

Test the fruit of what you see, hear, or feel by knowing that every good tree produces good fruit. When you have thoughts that are not coming from God and you want to know His will, plead the blood of Jesus over yourself and ask Him to take captive every thought to make it obedient to Christ. Know that if someone is not getting their power from Christ, then it is from the anti-christ. Seek discernment from the Holy Spirit. The Holy Spirit within you is stronger than anything you will encounter in this world.

> *We demolish arguments and every pretension that sets itself up against the knowledge of God, and we take captive every thought to make it obedient to Christ.* 2 Corinthians 10:5
>
> *[Jesus said] "Beware of false prophets, who come to you in sheep's clothing, but inwardly they are ravenous wolves. You will know them*

by their fruits. Do men gather grapes from thornbushes or figs from thistles? Even so, every good tree bears good fruit, but a bad tree bears bad fruit. A good tree cannot bear bad fruit, nor can a bad tree bear good fruit. Every tree that does not bear good fruit is cut down and thrown into the fire. Therefore by their fruits you will know them." Matthew 7:15–20 (NKJV)

Beloved, do not believe every spirit, but test the spirits, whether they are of God; because many false prophets have gone out into the world. By this you know the Spirit of God: Every spirit that confesses that Jesus Christ has come in the flesh is of God, and every spirit that does not confess that Jesus Christ has come in the flesh is not of God. And this is the spirit of the Antichrist, which you have heard was coming, and is now already in the world. You are of God, little children, and have overcome them, because He who is in you is greater than he who is in the world. 1 John 4:1–4 (NKJV)

My family and I were met with a lot of resistance from the enemy when we began attending the church that we attend. We had to test the fruit to determine the source. First, we had the hardest time getting to church. We felt condemnation of everything lacking at this start-up church and sometimes an overwhelming feeling that we did not belong there. Because there seemed to be so much negative resistance, we continued to go and see it through until we heard from God that this was not the church for us. Each time we went, we would see that the pastor was preaching the Word of God and he was producing good fruit. Now we are very engaged and useful to this new church and know that God wanted us there all along. Sometimes when you feel the most resistance, you can be sure you are working in God's will. A good rule of thumb is to be persistent, pray for discernment, and carry on until you hear otherwise from God. It isn't always about us, but sometimes rather how God can use us.

Journaling Exercise

1. Pray that God brings people into your life that produce good fruit. If you need to, pray that God brings you that special Christian friend that you need.

For You formed my inward parts; You wove me in my mother's womb.
Psalm 139:13 (NASB)

Lesson 29

JARS OF CLAY

We are created in the image of God. He sculpted each one of us individually and knows our inmost being. We cannot hide anything from Him, not even the number of hairs on our head. Think of the depths of understanding He has of us. He sees our sinful nature, yet He continues to mold us. He gently removes pieces that are displeasing to Him and He adds fine lines that resemble Jesus. We are the clay and He is the Potter. As we die to our flesh, we are being transformed into the image of Christ and our jars are filled with the light of life which is His Holy Spirit, the power of God.

Heavenly Father, I pray that You will speak to me through Your Word and provide divine understanding of Your truth. Give me ears to hear and eyes to see and a heart to understand. In Jesus' name I pray, amen.

Then the word of the LORD came to me; "O house of Israel, can I not do with you as this potter does?" declares the LORD. "Like clay in the hand of the potter, so are you in my hands, O house of Israel." *Jeremiah 18:5–6*

Yet, O LORD, you are our Father. We are the clay, you are the potter, we are all the work of your hand. *Isaiah 64:8*

For God, who said, "Let light shine out of darkness," made his light shine in our hearts to give us the light of the knowledge of the glory of God in the face of Christ. But we have this treasure in jars of clay

to show that this all-surpassing power is from God and not from us.
2 Corinthians 4:6–7

Because we are no longer in the dark, but the light, the blood of Jesus will wash clean our sins at every moment of the day: those sins known and unknown to us. We are forgiven for past, present, and future sins. This knowledge and peace of mind will allow the anointing of the Holy Spirit to work stronger in us to self-correct us and convict us to become more like Him. Jesus tells us that the voice of the Holy Spirit within us is His will being revealed to us. Jesus lives in us! We must welcome the Holy Spirit and invite Him to be present in us and around us.

But if we walk in the light, as he is in the light, we have fellowship with one another, and the blood of Jesus, his Son, purifies us from all sin.
1 John 1:7

As a teenager, I had an adult friend named Katie. I have lost touch with her, but I named my daughter after her. I remember her as a beautiful lady inside and out who loved to write poetry. On my sixteenth birthday, Katie gave me a card with a quote from an author who won the Nobel Peace Prize, Dag Hammarskjöld:

"If only I may grow firmer, simpler, quieter, warmer."

These words describe how the Holy Spirit speaks to you deep within you. The Spirit works inside us to show us our weaknesses and convicts us to become more like Christ and leads us into God's will for us. The Holy Spirit gently prompts you to do something, to change, and even what to pray. The next time you are praying alone or in a group— wait for the quiet whisper deep inside to reveal a word of what to pray for that person.

[Jesus said] "I still have many things to say to you, but you cannot bear them now. However, when He, the Spirit of truth, has come, He will guide you into all truth; for He will not speak on His own authority, but whatever He hears He will speak; and He will tell you things to

come. He will glorify Me, for He will take of what is Mine and declare it to you. All things that the Father has are Mine. Therefore I said that He will take of Mine and declare it to you." John 16:12–15 (NKJV)

Now we have received, not the spirit of the world, but the Spirit who is from God, that we might know the things that have been freely given to us by God. These things we also speak, not in words which man's wisdom teaches but which the Holy Spirit teaches, comparing spiritual things with spiritual. But the natural man does not receive the things of the Spirit of God, for they are foolishness to him; nor can he know them, because they are spiritually discerned. But he who is spiritual judges all things, yet he himself is rightly judged by no one. For "who has known the mind of the LORD that he may instruct Him?" But we have the mind of Christ. 1 Corinthians 2:12–16 (NKJV)

We have not received the spirit of the world but the Spirit who is from God, that we may understand what God has freely given us. This is what we speak, not in words taught us by human wisdom but in words taught by the Spirit, expressing spiritual truths in spiritual words. The man without the Spirit does not accept the things that come from the Spirit of God, for they are foolishness to him, and he cannot understand them, because they are spiritually discerned. The spiritual man makes judgments about all things, but he himself is not subject to any man's judgment: "For who has known the mind of the Lord that he may instruct him?" But we have the mind of Christ.
1 Corinthians 2:12–16

Journaling Exercise

1. Please listen online to the song by Gongor, "Beautiful Things" and write down your thoughts on how we are the clay and God is the Potter.

2. Please listen online to the song "Same Power" by Jeremy Camp. What powers does this song reveal that we have?

Into your hands I commit my spirit;
you have redeemed me, O LORD, faithful God.
Psalm 31:5 (ESV)

Lesson 30

BAPTIZED BY FIRE

How do we know if we have the Holy Spirit guiding us? We are called to be baptized by water for repentance and we are baptized by fire when the Holy Spirit comes upon us. When Jesus was baptized, the Holy Spirit descended, or came upon Him like a dove. When we are filled with the Spirit, we are able to be Spirit-led and Spirit-empowered.

Heavenly Father, I pray that You will speak to me through Your Word and provide divine understanding of Your truth. Give me ears to hear and eyes to see and a heart to understand. In Jesus' name I pray, amen.

Jesus answered, "I tell you the truth, no one can enter the kingdom of God unless he is born of water and the Spirit. Flesh gives birth to flesh, but the Spirit gives birth to spirit. You should not be surprised at my saying 'You must be born again'. The wind blows wherever it pleases. You hear its sounds, but you cannot tell where it comes from or where it is going. So it is with everyone born of the Spirit." *John 3: 5–8*

[Jesus said] "But you will receive power when the Holy Spirit has come upon you." *Acts 1:8a (ESV)*

[John the Baptist said] "I baptize you with water for repentance. But after me will come one who is more powerful than I, whose sandals I am not fit to carry. He will baptize you with the Holy Spirit and with fire. *Matthew 3:11*

We were sealed with the Holy Spirit when we accepted Jesus into our heart. This sealing of the Spirit and our salvation secured is usually different than the Holy Spirit coming upon you as in the day of Pentecost in the book of Acts. How and when the Spirit comes upon you is between you and God.

> *In him we were also chosen, having been predestined according to the plan of him who works out everything in conformity with the purpose of his will, in order that we, who were the first to hope in Christ, might be for the praise of his glory. And you also were included in Christ when you heard the word of truth, the gospel of your salvation. Having believed, you were marked in him with a seal, the promised Holy Spirit, who is a deposit guaranteeing our inheritance until the redemption of those who are God's possession-to the praise of his glory.* Ephesians 1:11–14
>
> *When the Day of Pentecost had fully come, they were all with one accord in one place. And suddenly there came a sound from heaven, as of a rushing mighty wind, and it filled the whole house where they were sitting. Then there appeared to them divided tongues, as of fire, and one sat upon each of them. And they were all filled with the Holy Spirit and began to speak with other tongues, as the Spirit gave them utterance.* Acts 2:1–4 (NKJV)

The Open Bible (NASB) instructs on how to be filled with the Holy Spirit. First, you must desire Him to fill you. Second, you must ask Him to fill you. Third, you must believe that He does fill you. The Holy Spirit is the "living water" that flows through us. The scripture references of these instructions are as follows:

> *Jesus answered "Everyone who drinks this water will be thirsty again, but whoever drinks the water I give him will never thirst. Indeed, the water I give him will become in him a spring of water welling up to eternal life."* John 4:13–14
>
> *On the last day, that great day of the feast, Jesus stood and cried out, saying, "If anyone thirsts, let him come to Me and drink. He who*

believes in Me, as the Scripture has said, out of his heart will flow rivers of living water." But this He spoke concerning the Spirit, whom those believing in Him would receive; for the Holy Spirit was not yet given, because Jesus was not yet glorified. John 7:37–39 (NKJV)

If you desire the Holy Spirit, you are called to ask to receive it. If you desire this, say this prayer that Paul prayed for the Ephesians. Invite the Spirit into your inner being.

For this reason I bow my knees before the Father, from whom every family in heaven and on earth is named, that according to the riches of his glory he may grant you to be strengthened with power through his Spirit in your inner being, so that Christ may dwell in your hearts through faith—that you, being rooted and grounded in love, may have strength to comprehend with all the saints what is the breadth and length and height and depth, and to know the love of Christ that surpasses knowledge, that you may be filled with all the fullness of God. (Ephesians 3:14–19) (ESV)

Now kneel and make this prayer personal for you:

For this reason I bow my knees before You, Father, from whom every family in heaven and on earth is named, that according to the riches of Your glory that You may grant me to be strengthened with power through Your Spirit in my inner being, so that Christ may dwell in my heart through faith—that I may be rooted and grounded in love, may have strength to comprehend with all the saints what is the breadth and length and height and depth, and to know the love of Christ that surpasses knowledge, that I may be filled with all the fullness of God. Amen.

Peter instructs us to repent, get baptized, and receive the Holy Spirit. Jesus, in John 14, promises the Holy Spirit to those that love Him and obey Him. We are called to be baptized out of obedience. Pray to see if it is your time to get baptized or re-baptized with the right heart for Jesus. Jesus showed us how to be baptized when He was fully submerged in the water.

[Jesus said] "If you love me, you will obey what I command. And I will ask the Father, and he will give you another Counselor to be with you forever—the Spirit of truth….Whoever has my commands and obeys them, he is the one who loves me. He who loves me will be loved by my Father, and I too will love him and show myself to him." John 14:15–17 and 21

Peter replied, "Repent and be baptized, every one of you, in the name of Jesus Christ for the forgiveness of your sins. And you will receive the gift of the Holy Spirit." Acts 2:38

I felt the Spirit come upon me as I was giving my testimony immediately before I was baptized. Right before I stepped on the platform of the altar, I stood behind the curtain praying that the Holy Spirit would shine on me so that it would be visible to my son in the audience and have a great impact on him. This is exactly what happened. I was very nervous as I began speaking to the large audience over a microphone. I felt the Holy Spirit shine on my head and ignite a pilot light inside me that calmed me and I began to give my testimony through God's grace and strength.

My husband and I went through a class about the Holy Spirit at an Assembly of God church in Ohio. Speaking in tongues is one of the signs that the Holy Spirit is indeed upon you and it is recorded in the Bible. (Read more of this in Acts 2:1–13 & 1 Corinthians 14.) Pastor Michael LoPresti laid his hands and prayed in his tongue and my husband began to speak words from the Holy Spirit that only God knows. This is a personal prayer language to speak to God of things in private that you don't even know you need to pray. The devil cannot understand it. As he laid his hands on me, I spoke a full sentence in Hebrew that was translated by someone who is a Jewish-Christian. My first word was "ra'ah", which in Hebrew means 'to see' or 'behold', and the rest of the sentence was a personal message from God. I still do not speak a private language but many times when I praise in song, my legs shake uncontrollably from the Spirit. When praying in the Spirit, my touch to someone can be very hot. A person can be "on fire" in their speech with passion or led by the Holy Spirit. God can do whatever He pleases for each individual. You will know it is not you, but the power of God.

For anyone who speaks in a tongue does not speak to men but to God. Indeed, no one understands him; he utters mysteries with his spirit. 1 Corinthians 14:2

And it happened, while Apollos was at Corinth, that Paul, having passed through the upper regions, came to Ephesus. And finding some disciples he said to them, "Did you receive the Holy Spirit when you believed?" So they said to him, "We have not so much as heard whether there is a Holy Spirit." And he said to them, "Into what then were you baptized?" So they said, "Into John's baptism." Then Paul said, "John indeed baptized with a baptism of repentance, saying to the people that they should believe on Him who would come after him, that is, on Christ Jesus." When they heard this, they were baptized in the name of the Lord Jesus. And when Paul had laid hands on them, the Holy Spirit came upon them, and they spoke with tongues and prophesied. Acts 19:1–6 (NKJV)

I thank God that I speak in tongues more than all of you. But in the church I would rather speak five intelligible words to instruct others than ten thousand words in tongue. 1 Corinthians 14:18–19

Therefore, my brothers, be eager to prophesy, and do not forbid speaking in tongues. But everything should be done in a fitting and orderly way. 1 Corinthians 14:39–40

The Holy Spirit can also be felt when you worship as a group of believers. Pray and invite the Holy Spirit to be present and fill the atmosphere of your church before the service starts. Ask that the Holy Spirit touch every person. Pray this until you feel the Spirit come in. It feels like a wind of peace settling in. When the Holy Spirit is very present, the air becomes very thick. Do not be afraid to lift your hands in complete surrender as you praise and worship. There is no reason to be ashamed of Jesus, we proclaim Him! When you've had a bad go of things, or even a fight on the way to church, praise Jesus even more while worshiping because you are so grateful that your righteousness comes from Him and not from you. Gratefulness is the right heart attitude when praising Jesus.

God tells us that He inhabits the praises of His people and the Holy Spirit flows with full surrender of praise. If you start to feel embarrassment, call all of your thoughts captive to the obedience of Jesus Christ. When I am singing in worship and stretch my arms up to Him, I also start praising Jesus with whispers like, "Lord Jesus, I praise Your Holy Name. You are the precious Lamb that was slayed for me." I imagine Jesus' arms stretched wide on the cross, sitting at His feet in the future, or dancing for Him. Sometimes I imagine praising with the angels saying, "Holy, holy holy is the LORD God Almighty who was and is and is to come." The Holy Spirit will inhabit your praises.

[Jesus said] "God is spirit, and his worshipers must worship in spirit and in truth." John 4:24

If anyone is ashamed of me and my words, the Son of Man will be ashamed of him when he comes in his glory and in the glory of the Father and of the holy angels. Luke 9:26

Therefore, since we are receiving a kingdom that cannot be shaken, let us be thankful, and so worship God acceptably with reverence and awe, for our "God is a consuming fire." Hebrews 12:28–29

May my prayer be counted as incense before You; The lifting up of my hands as the evening offering. Psalm 141:2 (NASB)

I will praise you as long as I live, and in your name I will lift up my hands. Psalm 63:4

My heart is steadfast, O God; I will sing, I will sing praises, even with my soul. Psalm 108:1 (NASB)

Journaling Exercise

1. Listen online to the song "Holy Spirit You Are Welcome Here" by Kim Walker Smith, "Oceans" by Hillsong United and "Your Glory/Nothing but the Blood" by All Sons and Daughters. Raise your hands full in praise and feel the Holy Spirit.

2. While praying at a Woman of Worship gathering, Jesus showed me a vision of what heaven looks like. I do not remember His face, but I remember the landscape and that He smiled, gestured slightly with His hands and said without speaking, "Let's dance." If you would like to download this image of Jesus in heaven, go to www.aspiritualjourneytoGodsbest.com. Be bold and get up and dance for Jesus. Listen online to "Come to Jesus" by Chris Rice.

3. Explain what you felt when praising Jesus.

Let them thank the LORD for his steadfast love,
for his wondrous works to the children of man!
Psalm 107:15 (ESV)

Lesson 31

A HOLY TEMPLE

ur body is a temple that houses the Holy Spirit. We must honor it by taking care of it so that we might be healthy and able to do God's will. We are a vessel for God to use for holy works. The Bible calls us to have self-control, or moderation, in all aspects of our lives, including our bodies. Self-control, or self-discipline, is one of the nine traits of the fruit of the Spirit.

We are not our own, but were bought at a great price by Jesus at Calvary. God loves us the same without any partiality to skin type, facial features, wages earned, or body type. He beautifully loves us for just being us. In 1 Samuel 16, it says that God judges the heart, where man judges the outward appearance. On the flip side, the Bible also tells us to honor God with our body. He expects us to be good stewards of what He has given us; to love the gift that He has given us. We were made in His image.

If you suffer in this area, look closely and see if the devil is not having a field day with you by bringing condemnation. If so, he's messing with you and bringing on shame. The devil would love to disable you and keep you distracted on any other issue than doing God's will. Recognizing the source is the beginning. Resist by saying, "There is no condemnation for those that are in Christ Jesus, so get behind me, Satan." The next time you see someone who looks so fit and healthy and is not a Christian; remember that the enemy is not going to bother condemning them if he knows he has them.

For some, gluttony is an issue. I confess that my weakness, or sinful nature where the devil tries to condemn me, is a lack of self-discipline, or laziness to exercise on a regular basis. I stay somewhat active, but Lord have mercy on me, I do not like to make myself exercise. In the book of James, it says to confess your sins, pray for one another, and be healed. Bring your weakness out of the darkness and into the light with the help of a trusted Christian friend. Buddy up and work on it together by encouraging each other. There is victory in doing what you do not want to do.

Examine yourself to see if you have given all of your internal hurts to Jesus to be healed. Ask Him to help by giving you the desire to do what you should and persevere. Jesus can heal the hearts of murderers like the Apostle Paul and uses them for great works. We should never limit His powers to set us free. Romans 8:36 tells us, "So if the Son sets you free, you will be free indeed." Don't believe the lies that the father of all lies is trying to put in you right now. We are beautifully wrapped in Jesus' righteous garment of jewels and, oh, how He loves you.

There is a hole in all of us that can only be filled by God. Devour His word by reading your Bible. Spend time with Him and praise His Holy Name. He promises to renew our youth like the eagle's and restore the years that the locusts have taken away.

Heavenly Father, I pray that You will speak to me through Your Word and provide divine understanding of Your truth. Give me ears to hear and eyes to see and a heart to understand. In Jesus' name I pray, amen.

But the LORD said to Samuel, "Do not consider his appearance or his height, for I have rejected him. The LORD does not look at the things man looks at. Man looks at the outward appearance, but the LORD looks at the heart." *1 Samuel 16:7*

Do you not know that your body is a temple of the Holy Spirit, who is in you, whom you have received from God? You are not your own; you were bought at a price. Therefore honor God with your body. *1 Corinthians 6:19–20*

Like a city whose walls are broken down is a man who lacks self-control. *Proverbs 25:28*

His divine power has granted to us all things that pertain to life and godliness, through the knowledge of him who called us to his own glory and excellence, by which he has granted to us his precious and very great promises, so that through them you may become partakers of the divine nature, having escaped from the corruption that is in the world because of sinful desire. For this very reason, make every effort to supplement your faith with virtue, and virtue with knowledge, and knowledge with self-control, and self-control with steadfastness, and steadfastness with godliness, and godliness with brotherly affection, and brotherly affection with love. For if these qualities are yours and are increasing, they keep you from being ineffective or unfruitful in the knowledge of our Lord Jesus Christ. 2 Peter 1:3–8 (ESV)

Bless the LORD, O my soul, and all that is within me, bless his holy name! Bless the LORD, O my soul, and forget not all his benefits, who forgives all your iniquity, who heals all your diseases, who redeems your life from the pit, who crowns you with steadfast love and mercy, who satisfies you with good so that your youth is renewed like the eagle's. Psalm 103:1–5 (ESV)

"So I will restore to you the years that the swarming locust has eaten, the crawling locust, the consuming locust, and the chewing locust, my great army which I sent among you." Joel 2:25–32 (NKJV)

A Living Sacrifice

Our body is a vessel that God can use in remarkable ways. Because God gave each of us free will, we must voluntarily offer our bodies for His use. Before offering your body as a vessel, ask God to examine your heart and remove anything that is not pleasing to Him, so that you may be used for holy works. Once you have asked Him to examine your heart, offer your body to your heavenly Father as a living sacrifice and a vessel for Him to use as He pleases. Every time I use the prayer below, God uses me during that day. God will use you if you offer yourself to Him. Imagine the power of Christians throughout the world if we all offered ourselves to do His good and perfect will each day!

Heavenly Father, I pray that You will speak to me through Your word and provide divine understanding of Your truth. Give me ears to hear and eyes to see and a heart to understand. In Jesus' name I pray, amen.

Teach me to do your will, for you are my God; may your good Spirit lead me on level ground. *Psalm 143:10*

I beseech you therefore, brethren, by the mercies of God, that you <u>present your bodies a living sacrifice</u>, holy, acceptable to God, which is your reasonable service. And do not be conformed to this world, but be transformed by the renewing of your mind, that you may prove what is the good and acceptable and <u>perfect will of God</u>. *Romans 12:1–2 (NKJV)*

Therefore, if anyone cleanses himself from what is dishonorable, he will be a vessel for honorable use, set apart as holy, useful to the master of the house, ready for every good work. *2 Timothy 2:21 (ESV)*

A Daily Prayer for Doing God's Work

Heavenly Father, I pray the armor of God on so that I may stand firm. I pray the Helmet of Salvation and the Breastplate of Righteousness secure on my chest. Gird my loins with the Truth and shod my feet with the Preparation of the Gospel of Peace. In one hand I wield the Shield of Faith to resist all fiery darts of the enemy, and the other the Sword of the Spirit which is the Word of God, sharper than any two-edged sword. In Jesus' name I pray the armor of God on and plead the blood of Jesus over me for protection. I loose anything not from Jesus and I bind all my thoughts captive to the obedience of Jesus Christ. God did not give me a spirit of fear, but power, love, and a sound mind.

I thank you, Father, for allowing me to be Your child and I am so grateful that You love me and will always be there for me. Please examine my heart and if anything is displeasing to You or if there is anyone I need to forgive, show me so that I may repent. [pause and repent]

Heavenly Father, I offer my body today as a living sacrifice to do Your good and perfect will. May I be a vessel for You to use for holy works. I pray for spiritual wisdom and revelation from You, LORD. I ask that my thoughts be Your thoughts and my words be Your words. Please close my mouth to what I am not supposed to say. May the words of my mouth and meditation of my heart be pleasing in Your sight and may I glorify You, LORD.

I die to myself today and live for You, Jesus. I am not my own, but was bought at a great price. I claim the victory of this day, because You have already overcome the world for us. Please shine Your light through me, Jesus. Give me Your eyes to see people as You see them and Your heart to love them as You love them. Fill me with Your grace.

Holy Spirit, You are welcome here and I ask that You be present in me and give me utterance.

This is the day the LORD has made, let us rejoice and be glad! I pray this all in Jesus' precious name, amen.

Journaling Exercise

1. Confess your weaknesses in regards to your body and ask Jesus for help. If you are in a group, pray for one another to be loosed from any bonds that keep you from doing what you should and call you minds captive to the obedience of Jesus Christ. Ask for His strength, for when we are weak, He is strong.

2. For the next week, say the Daily Prayer above in the morning and write how God used you to do His holy works.

He is like a tree planted by steams of water that yields its fruit in its season,
and its leaf does not wither. In all that he does, he prospers.
Psalm 1:3 (ESV)

Lesson 32
SPIRITUAL GIFTS

The Lord has given each of us certain spiritual gifts that manifest from the Holy Spirit that dwells within us and we need only call on them. Everyone is unique in their spiritual gifting and they combine with others as the body of Christ to do God's work on earth. Measure the gifts given to you by how much you are helping the body of Christ and doing the works that God calls us to do. Our gifts, or talents, are given to us so that we might use them to glorify God and be able to accomplish what He has planned for us to do before we were even born. Remember that we are told that "from everyone who has been given much, much will be demanded; and from the one who has been entrusted with much, much more will be asked." (Luke 12:48b) If God puts someone in your life so that you can use the gifts that He has given you, try to be obedient and help that person.

Heavenly Father, I pray that You speak to me through Your Word and provide divine understanding of Your truth. Give me ears to hear and eyes to see and a heart to understand. In Jesus' name I pray, Amen.

But to each one is given the manifestation of the Spirit for the common good. For to one is given the word of wisdom through the Spirit, and to another the word of knowledge according to the same Spirit; to another faith by the same Spirit, and to another gifts of healing by the one Spirit, and to another the effecting of miracles, and to another prophecy, and

to another the distinguishing of spirits, to another various kinds of tongues, and to another the interpretation of tongues. But one and the same Spirit works all these things, distributing to each one individually just as He wills. 1 Corinthians 12:7–11 (NASB)

Since we have gifts that differ according to the grace given to us, each of us is to exercise them accordingly: if prophecy, according to the proportion of his faith; if service, in his serving; or he who teaches, in his teaching; or he who exhorts, in his exhortation; he who gives, with liberality; he who leads, with diligence; he who shows mercy, with cheerfulness. Romans 12:6–8 (NASB)

Now you are the body of Christ, and each one of you is a part of it. And in the church God has appointed first of all apostles, second prophets, third teachers, then workers of miracles, also those having gifts of healing, those able to help others, those with gifts of administration, and those speaking in different kinds of tongues. 1 Corinthians 12:27–28

Pursue love, yet desire earnestly spiritual gifts, but especially that you may prophesy. For one who speaks in a tongue does not speak to men but to God; for no one understands, but in his spirit he speaks mysteries. But one who prophesies speaks to men for edification and exhortation and consolation. One who speaks in a tongue edifies himself; but one who prophesies edifies the church. 1 Corinthians 14:1–4 (NASB)

Praise be to the God and Father of our Lord Jesus Christ, who has blessed us in the heavenly realms with every spiritual blessing in Christ. Ephesians 1:3

…All the days ordained for me were written in your book before one of them came to be. Psalm 139:16

We are all called to pray for one another. Some have a natural gifting from God and are called to be prayer warriors and intercede for others that need prayer. This is called being an intercessor. A burden is placed on your heart to pray for a certain person. God is calling you to stand in the gap between the person that you are concerned for and Him. Your faith can stand in the gap for them with Jesus' help. Most likely this person is under attack from Satan and you must take up the sword of God's Word and fight for them. It is very effective to have a prayer partner or a group that you can give the prayer request to for immediate intercession. I have known intercessors to pray the entire day for one person. To avoid attack before beginning to intercede for another, always place the armor of God on yourself first and those who are praying with you. Pray for your family members to be protected as well. God called me to use this prayer below for a son of a friend whom I did not know at that very moment was being resuscitated by paramedics from attempted suicide. There is so much power in prayer.

Prayer of Intercession against Spiritual Warfare

Holy, Holy, Holy, is the Lord God Almighty; we praise Your Great Name.

Heavenly Father, because we have a high priest that sits at Your right hand that was perfectly blameless and died for us, we have the confidence to approach the throne of grace and ask to receive mercy for_____. Father, we thank you that You always hear our prayers. We stand in the gap for _____ with our faith.

Your Word is living and active and sharper than any two-edged sword, able to separate the soul and the spirit and the joints from the marrow. We claim the power of Your Word over this prayer. It is written that the "fervent, effectual prayer of a righteous man availeth much, and we ask that You hear our petitions and have mercy on_____.

We lift up _____ to Your throne and ask that You hide_____ in the secret place of the Most High and allow_____ to rest under the shadow of the Almighty. Protect _____ under Your wings where ___ may find refuge.

The book of Revelation tells us that the enemy was overcome by the blood of the Lamb. Jesus, you have delivered us from the power of darkness with Your blood. We plead the precious blood of Jesus poured over _____. We claim Your mighty resurrection power to be upon _____ and we ask that a hedge of protection be also placed around_____. You are the light that brought light to us all and we ask that Your light surround and engulf_____. Where Your light is, Jesus, there can be no darkness.

At the name of Jesus every knee should bow, of things in heaven, and things on earth, and things under the earth. We claim the power of Your Mighty Name over all principalities of darkness that come against _____ *and that no weapons formed against* _____*shall prosper.*

Perfect love casts out all fear. We claim Your perfect love over _____, *Jesus. We ask that all* _____ *thoughts be held captive to the obedience of Jesus Christ. May the peace of the Lord be upon* _____, *a peace that surpasses all understanding and guards our hearts and minds in Christ Jesus.*

Jesus, please send down mighty warrior angels to guard and protect _____. *"If God is for us, who can be against us?" We thank you LORD for Your promises and we praise Your Mighty Name. We pray this all in the precious name of Jesus, amen.*

Journaling Exercise

1. God will put someone on your heart that needs prayer. Try using the above prayer if that person is under a lot of duress.

2. Practice seeking the Holy Spirit by waiting in the silence for what to pray and calling on the Spirit to be present in your church. Describe the outcome.

3. If you do not know your spiritual gifts, you can go online and take a test. Search engine: Assembly of God spiritual gifts test. Your gifting(s) can change according to the season that God has for you. What spiritual gifts has God given you?

WEEK 8
GROUP QUESTIONS

1. Discuss how we might "abide" in Jesus.

2. What does it mean to be "Baptized by Fire"?

3. If you have any issues with control of your body, share them. Pray for each other and be healed. Encourage each other throughout the week.

4. Do you know what spiritual gifts God has given you?

5. Was anyone able to use the prayer against Spiritual Warfare?

6. What was the result of using the Daily Prayer above? If you didn't get a chance to use the prayer, use it and report back to the group your results next week.

Week 9

A CHRIST-CENTERED LIFE

I will meditate on your precepts and fix my eyes on your ways.
I will delight in your statutes; I will not forget your word.
Psalm 119:15–16 (ESV)

Lesson 33

A Servant's Heart

At some point in our transformation, we are called to be the hands and feet of Jesus. Sometimes we are Mary and other times we are Martha. In other words, sometimes we must sit at Jesus' feet and sometimes we must serve others in His name. In order to be able to serve others, we must first go to our special place and rest in Jesus and be filled up by Him. The same is true after you serve. If you don't do this, you *will* get worn out and grumpy. Jesus modeled this need when He went away from His disciples and spent private time with His Father. Ask Jesus to "anoint you with the oil of joy" until your "cup overflows" (Psalm 45:7 & Psalm 23:5). Out of the abundance of Jesus' love and grace comes a servant's heart.

As a good servant, we are called to be doers of the Word. We need to have faith with action and the humility required to truly serve our Lord Jesus. God will reveal to each of us what He has called us to do for the Kingdom. Not everyone can do great things. But, as Mother Teresa said, "We can all do small things with great love."

One place that I thought I could never go to serve was Africa. I was afraid of areas of great poverty and potential violence. One Sunday in church I was praising Jesus with my eyes closed and He revealed to me how to have the ability to go where you think you cannot go. He showed me a poor child in Africa through His loving eyes. I thought, "Oh, so that's how you go." We do it out of *His* love.

Heavenly Father, I pray that You will speak to me through Your Word and provide divine understanding of Your truth. Give me ears to hear and eyes to see and a heart to understand. In Jesus' name I pray, amen.

For we are God's workmanship, created in Christ Jesus to do good works, which God prepared in advance for us to do. *Ephesians 2:10*

And calling them to Himself, Jesus said to them, "You know that those who are recognized as rulers of the Gentiles lord it over them; and their great men exercise authority over them. But it is not so among you, but whoever wishes to become great among you shall be your servant; and whoever wishes to be first among you shall be slave of all. For even the Son of Man did not come to be served, but to serve, and to give His life a ransom for many." *Mark 10:42–45 (NASB)*

And sitting down, He called the twelve and said to them, "If anyone wants to be first, he shall be last of all, and servant of all." *Mark 9:35 (NASB)*

"The King will reply, 'I tell you the truth, whatever you did for one of the least of these brothers of mine, you did for me.'" *Matthew 25:40*

[Jesus said] "When the Son of Man comes in his glory, and all the angels with him, then he will sit on his glorious throne. Before him will be gathered all the nations, and he will separate people one from another as a shepherd separates the sheep from the goats. And he will place the sheep on his right, but the goats on the left. Then the King will say to those on his right, 'Come, you who are blessed by my Father, inherit the kingdom prepared for you from the foundation of the world. For I was hungry and you gave me food, I was thirsty and you gave me drink, I was a stranger and you welcomed me, I was naked and you clothed me, I was sick and you visited me, I was in prison and you came to me.'" *Matthew 25:31–36 (ESV)*

You foolish man, do you want evidence that faith without deeds is useless? Was not our ancestor Abraham considered righteous for what he did when he offered his son Isaac on the altar? You see that his faith

and his actions were working together, and his faith was made complete by what he did. James 2:20–22

Do nothing from selfish ambition or conceit, but in humility count others more significant than yourselves. Let each of you look not only to his own interests, but also to the interests of others. Have this mind among yourselves, which is yours in Christ Jesus, who, though he was in the form of God, did not count equality with God a thing to be grasped, but emptied himself, by taking the form of a servant, being born in the likeness of men. And being found in human form, he humbled himself by becoming obedient to the point of death, even death on a cross. Philippians 2:3–8 (ESV)

"In everything I did, I showed you that by this kind of hard work we must help the weak, remembering the words the Lord Jesus himself said: 'It is more blessed to give than to receive.'" Acts 20:35

Religion that is pure and undefiled before God, the Father, is this: to visit orphans and widows in their affliction, and to keep oneself unstained from the world. James 1:27(ESV)

Defend the poor and the fatherless; do justice to the afflicted and needy. Deliver the poor and the needy; free them from the hand of the wicked. They do not know, nor do they understand; they walk about in darkness; all the foundations of the earth are unstable. Psalm 82:3–5 (NKJV)

We simply must trust and obey when God reveals something to us through the Holy Spirit within us. When He tells us to do something, we must be brave and obedient. Written below are instances where two women heard from God and obeyed. The more you trust and obey, the greater God will use you. From experience I have learned to not do more than God asks, but exactly what He asks. The results are up to Him. The secret is to pray and obey.

But Samuel replied: "Does the LORD delight in burnt offerings and sacrifices as much as in obeying the voice of the LORD? To obey is better than sacrifice, and to heed is better than the fat of rams." 1 Samuel 15:22

[Jesus said] For everyone who has will be given more, and he will have an abundance. Whoever does not have, even what he has will be taken from him. And throw that worthless servant outside, into the darkness, where there will be weeping and gnashing of teeth.
Matthew 25:29–30

By Roberta

The only time I have audibly heard God say something to me was when He said, "Call your hairdresser." I thought, "I don't need a haircut and I have no idea what I'm supposed to say." I heard Him say it again. I didn't want to call him because I didn't know him very well, only that he cut my hair. His lifestyle was that of a homosexual and he struggled with drugs and alcohol. He thought he was born to have a relationship with men, but he still said he loved Jesus. The third time I heard Him, I knew it was God and I knew I had to call. Finally, I called him. I was hoping that I would get a recording. He picked up the phone and I asked him if he was busy. "No, I just had a cancellation and I am folding towels." I began by telling him what God had said to me. He burst into tears and told me that he was planning on killing himself that night. We cried together and I told him, "You just got a phone call from God and He loves you enough to prevent this." Praise God!

By Christine

I love it when I hear from God, but my favorite story is when someone else heard from God, and obeyed. One day my dad and I were visiting in my kitchen. It was close to my mom's birthday. (She passed away four years ago.) I expressed to my dad what I missed most about Mom. She would always tell me, "I'm really proud of you." It made me feel great. And that's what I missed from her most. About a week later I was at a worship service. During the singing time the lady next to me leaned over and whispered in my ear. It was odd, because I did not know her and she did not know me. She whispered, "I don't know your relationship with your mom, but I need to tell you she's really proud of you." That's right, the exact same words! God has perfect timing and is never late. I cried at first, because it touched me so, then I laughed with joy. Thank God! Little simple obedience can grow into big obedience. It brings Jesus joy and us too.

Sometimes God uses us to bless others with our time, talents, or treasure. We have to remember that it is His grace that abounds, not ours. We shouldn't get a big head or think we didn't get the right accolades or feel animosity, jealousy, or envy. Honestly, I have reacted this way and God had to correct my thoughts. Instead, we should feel honored that He would use us to bestow His gifts. It is by God's works through us that they will know Him. It is our joy to honor Him. Keep serving, keep loving, all who God places in your path.

We do not know God's plans for us. That is why we must seek His will and offer ourselves to be His servant. Oswald Chambers wrote in "My Utmost for His Highest," "God places his saints where they will bring the most glory to Him, and we are totally incapable of judging where that may be." It is not about trying to figure out where we are the most useful to Him, but just staying close to Him and seeking His will.

As Christians, we are called to mature from being only spiritually fed with milk and get to the meat of being useful in service. Charles Spurgeon writes in "Morning by Morning" "Some Christians are all for living on Christ but are not nearly as eager to live for Christ. Earth is simply preparation for heaven, and heaven will be where the saints will feast the most but will also serve the most. We will sit at the table of our Lord and will serve Him day and night in His temple, eating heavenly food and rendering perfect service." Awesome!

Many times we are called to hear what is burdening others. In prayer, we must petition for them by bringing their burdens to Jesus. Cry out to Him. In faith, we know that He hears our prayer. In faith, we know that He can at any point make our prayer requests happen. His will, not ours. We are just required to ask in faith. This knowledge will help you to not feel so overwhelmed when helping others. When you are feeling the heavy burden of so many needs, it works very well to listen online to the song "I Surrender All" and give each burden to Jesus. His yoke is easy and His burdens are light.

When our days on this earth are over, and we go to see our Maker, if only He might say: "You fought the good fight, you finished the race, and you have kept the faith, now there is in store for you the crown of righteousness…" (2 Timothy 4:7–8a)

As I was wrapping up this book, I met Rev. Edna Bjork through a mutual friend. She was in women's prison ministry for over twenty years and at the age of 65 began going over to India to spread the gospel. She told of healings, deliverances, casting out demons, and helping the poor learn about Jesus. Edna tells them that they must never put God in a box for He is infinite. The emotional and physical barriers she had to overcome while growing up are heart-wrenching. Her heart was healed by Jesus and she truly is a servant for the Lord. If you would like to read more about her missionary work and how she listens to the Holy Spirit, you can purchase her short book, "Will You Go?" online. Another book that I recently read was "Kisses from Katie" by Katie J. Davis. This is such a beautiful story of an 18 year old who heard God's calling for her to go to Uganda and she answered. If you haven't already read it, you will be amazed at what one young lady can do for His Kingdom.

A Prayer to Serve

Lord Jesus, anoint my head with Your oil of joy until my cup overflows with Your grace. For it is by Your grace I have been saved and by Your grace I have been forgiven much. Please break my heart, Lord, for what breaks Yours and give me Your eyes to see them as you see them. May I be able to extend Your love and grace today. In the precious name of Jesus I pray, amen.

Journaling Exercise

1. In order to want to serve Jesus, we need to absorb in our hearts how much He loves us. Read "Song of Solomon" in the Bible as a love letter from Jesus, the Bridegroom. "You are beautiful, my darling." He loves you for you.

2. Please listen online to "Here's My Heart" by David Crowder Band, "Lord I'm Ready Now" by Plumb, and "Hosanna" by Hillsong United. Ask Jesus to help break your heart for what breaks His.

3. Seek to know what God intends you to do for Him. Ask God to "open the door" and show you. The next step might be a time of training to prepare you or perhaps you have been in the fire being honed for His work. We can serve right here, right now, by helping our neighbors. Have a conversation with Him as you would your best friend. The dots of your life will begin to connect to reveal the plans He has for you.

For the LORD is good; his steadfast love endures forever,
and his faithfulness to all generations.
Psalm 100:5 (ESV)

Lesson 34
STRONGHOLDS IN MARRIAGE

*T*he only stronghold that we should have is Jesus being our rock eternal. Unfortunately, many times we have strongholds from the enemy. These strongholds are weapons against us that the devil is intentionally using to prevent us from following God's Word and prospering. A stronghold happens when Satan dominates your thinking in a certain aspect of your life. Marriage can easily fall prey to strongholds. I married my husband at the age of 23 and had no idea that day how rough and rocky the road was ahead. The heartache of miscarriages, fighting, stressful jobs, and a lack of communication took their toll. For some of these years, we were more like strangers than a couple. We came to two breaking points in our marriage and walking away. Most likely we would have separated the second time except we finally obeyed the instructions in the Bible about how to have a godly marriage. Today we now have the closeness that comes when your marriage is Christ-centered. If your marriage is in trouble, there is hope.

God knows that women, in their sinful nature, want to rebel against their husband's authority. Equally, men in their sinful nature do not want to love their wife as much as themselves. The devil wants to have a hand in ruining Christian marriages because they are supposed to be the ultimate reflection of what is right. An example of a stronghold might be bad experiences in a woman's life that make her not trust men and therefore she has a hard time submitting to her husband, as instructed in Ephesians 5, Colossians 3, and 1Peter 3. Many times it is hard for a man to love his wife as much as himself, for whom he should be willing to die, because of a stronghold of selfishness. The devil puts experiences in our lives to prevent a healthy love/respect relationship which sets the foundation that a marriage needs. Resist the devil and follow God's Word.

A healthy marriage should reflect the relationship of Jesus and His church. Women represent the church that submits in love to Christ. Men represent the sacrificial love that Jesus has for the people of the church. Once the husband starts seeing the respect that he desires, the wife will also see the love that she equally desires. The husband is considered the head and priest of the family as well as the protector. You will find his prayers to have a lot of power. It is very important to make Christ the center of your marriage by praying out loud for each other every evening and morning. Pray that your spouse will be blessed by the Lord and helped in what he/she might need. Your marriage will have a bond that cannot be broken. By serving each other with love and respect, our marriages will be a reflection of Christ that shines brightly in a world that needs to see Christ's love. It is by our actions that people will seek to know the Lord.

Heavenly Father, I pray that You will speak to me through Your Word and provide divine understanding of Your truth. Give me ears to hear and eyes to see and a heart to understand. In Jesus' name I pray, amen.

The LORD God fashioned into a woman the rib which He had taken from the man, and brought her to the man. The man said, "This is now bone of my bones, and flesh of my flesh; She shall be called Woman, because she was taken out of Man." For this reason a man shall leave his father and his mother, and be joined to his wife; and they shall become one flesh. Genesis 2:22–24 (NASB)

A wife of noble character who can find? She is worth far more than rubies. Her husband has full confidence in her and lacks nothing of value. She brings him good, not harm, all the days of her life. Proverbs 31:10–12

Wives submit to your husbands as to the Lord. For the husband is the head of the wife as Christ is the head of the church, his body, of which he is the Savior. Now as the church submits to Christ, so also wives should submit to their husbands in everything. Ephesians 5:22–24

Husbands, love your wives, just as Christ also loved the church and gave Himself up for her, so that He might sanctify her, having cleansed her by the washing of water with the word, that He might present to Himself the church in all her glory, having no spot or wrinkle or any such thing; but that she would be holy and blameless. So husbands ought also to love their own wives as their own bodies. He who loves his own wife loves himself; for no one ever hated his own flesh, but nourishes and cherishes it, just as Christ also does the church, because we are members of His body. For this reason a man shall leave his father and mother and shall be joined to his wife, and the two shall become one flesh. This mystery is great; but I am speaking with reference to Christ and the church. Nevertheless, each individual among you also is to love his own wife even as himself, and the wife must see to it that she respects her husband.
Ephesians 5:25–33 (NASB)

The book of Esther tells of a young Jewish woman who completely submitted to the authority of her older cousin that adopted her and then to the king that she married. Through her perfect example of submission, she was able to save the condemned Jewish people in all the provinces. The book of Ruth is a very good example of the submission of Ruth and the love from the Lord that Boaz had for her. Boaz's mother was Rahab, a prostitute who helped the two Jewish spies in Jericho, and Ruth was a Moabite from a tribe of notoriously very sinful people. Together Jesus' bloodline comes from these people.

Submitting to the authority of my husband was not easy. This is one part of the Bible where I truly thought the Apostle Paul was wrong. I remember two elderly ladies in Bible study telling me that I must do what was instructed and see how much my marriage would flourish. I resisted it, but their words planted a seed in my mind. I am ashamed to admit it, but at one point in our marriage the waiter would give me the bill because I was so controlling. A funny story was when I bought something with roosters on it and a friend told me women who have roosters in their kitchen like to rule the roost. There was truth in that for me, so I had to get rid of that theme.

For many of the 24 years of our marriage, my husband would say that he got no respect at home. He always was faithful and loved me greatly even though many times I felt ignored and low on his priorities. Many marriages go astray in these circumstances. God has been patient with my control issues and unkind words towards my husband. I have been very rebellious in this area. Below are the two verses that convicted me that I really needed to change in order to honor God.

> *Her husband has full confidence in her and lacks nothing of value. She brings him good, not harm, all the days of her life. Proverbs 31:11–12*
> *So that they may encourage the young women to love their husbands, to love their children, to be sensible, pure, workers at home, kind, being subject to their own husbands, so that the word of God will not be dishonored. Titus 2:4–5 (NASB)*

Now I pray that my husband receives spiritual wisdom and revelation from God to make the right decisions. Each morning I pray the armor of God on him, ask for him to receive wisdom from God, for Jesus to work through him, and I ask for favor from those he comes in contact with. We pray together to come to agreement on small decisions and for the big decisions, I pray that my husband hears God's voice as He directs our path.Our relationship is strengthened when we carve out time in the morning to read a daily devotion and a passage from the Bible. A recipe for a happy man: prepared food when possible, the T.V. remote, respect, do the small errands he asks, keep your phone charged, pray together daily, and intimacy. In return, a loving husband that wants to please you too. I can honestly say that I resisted and even resented every single one of these tasks in my sinful nature and since I have started making them a priority, our marriage has flourished. I praise God for those wise ladies in Bible study that mentored me.

"The 5 Love Languages" by Dr. Gary Chapman is a helpful book to read as a couple. My husband's love languages are touching and affirmation. I am working on complimenting what he does well and snuggling with him. My love languages are quality time and service. His act of service of making coffee in the morning makes me feel loved. I can tell my husband, "I would really appreciate it if you spent quality time with me and go for a walk in the park." He gets it now. The last of the five love languages is gift giving.

I know of one stronghold in our marriage that I had that was actually a generational curse. I confessed that I had an issue about sex while I was fasting and praying. Very soon after this confession, my pastor preached a sermon that blew my mind as I heard the truth spoken. The verse was "for this reason a man will leave his father and mother and be united to his wife, and they will become one flesh." This is the act of actually becoming "one", literally. This intimacy reflects the oneness of the Trinity. God gave us sex as a gift to reflect the oneness of the Trinity in our marriage. That is why it is a holy act. He went on to say that God created us to be sexual before the fall of Adam. Sex is not sinful, but rather sacred to the marriage bed. This was information that opened my eyes to the truth.

Marriage is entered into with a covenant between the couple and God. I always cry at weddings and now I know that it is because the Holy Spirit is present during this sacred ceremony. There was only one wedding that I attended that I felt nothing as they said their own vows and God was never mentioned throughout the ceremony. Traditional wedding vows between the couple and God are important.

The Bible instructs us to let no man or woman come between them and to honor this covenant relationship they have entered. God tells us that He hates divorce as well as violence. If you have divorced, ask for forgiveness and go forward with the knowledge that God has forgiven you. Before I knew Christ intimately, I came close to divorcing my husband and was tempted to be unfaithful as well. I thank God that He gave me a way out to not be unfaithful. I was convicted when I learned that when someone looks at you lustfully that they are committing adultery. Don't let their sin become your sin or to bring on condemnation. If this leering continues, share it with your mate and perhaps a close friend and God will take care of the problem. Satan will have no foothold. There is so much tempting in this world of debauchery and we must stand firm on God's instructions and lean on Jesus to be the person He wants us to be.

Marriage should be honored by all, and the marriage bed kept pure, for God will judge the adulterer and all the sexually immoral. Hebrews 13:4
Has not the LORD made them one? In flesh and spirit they are his. And why one? Because he was seeking godly offspring. So guard yourself in your spirit. And do not break faith with the wife of your youth. "I hate divorce," says the LORD God of Israel, "and I hate a

man's covering himself with violence as well as with his garment," says the LORD Almighty. So guard yourself in your spirit, and do not break faith. Malachi 2:15–16

No temptation has overtaken you but such as is common to man; and God is faithful, who will not allow you to be tempted beyond what you are able, but with the temptation will provide a way of escape also, that you may be able to endure it. 1 Corinthians 10:13 (NASB)

Ponder this response from the "Director" to a disillusioned woman named Jane who had only been married for six months in "That Hideous Strength" by C.S. Lewis, "They would say," he answered, "that you do not fail in obedience through lack of love, but have lost love because you never attempted obedience."

Journaling Exercise

1. Write down things that you can do to show love and respect. It must begin with you, even if your spouse does not know the Lord. God honors your obedience and will work on your spouse. If you are a man, begin to show acts of love that reflect Christ's love for you.

Teach me, O LORD, the way of Your statutes,
And I shall observe it to the end.
Psalm 119:33 (NASB)

Lesson 35

CHRISTIAN HOUSEHOLDS

Biblical Rules for Christian Households

1. Wives, submit to the authority of your husband acknowledging that he is head of the household and see what fruit it brings forth. (Ephesians 5:22–24)

2. Husbands, love your wives with the sacrificial love of Jesus Christ. (Ephesians 5:25–33)

3. Fathers, have the proper authority according to each child's needs to keep chaos out of the house and sin from reigning within.

4. Fathers, make sure your children are growing up in the training and instruction of the Lord. The book of Proverbs instructs youth in the wisdom of God's ways.

5. Children, honor and obey your parents and live a long fruitful life. (Deuteronomy 5:16)

6. Make it a family custom to go to church and pray together.

7. If a house is divided against itself, that house cannot stand. (Mark 3:24) Do not let your children come between you and your spouse: stand united.

8. Our words matter. (Matthew 5:22)

9. Mercy triumphs over judgment. (James 2:13)

10. Above all, love each other deeply, because love covers over a multitude of sins. (1 Peter 4:8)

Heavenly Father, I pray that You will speak to me through Your Word and provide divine understanding of Your truth. Give me ears to hear and eyes to see and a heart to understand. In Jesus' name I pray, amen.

Wives, be subject to your husbands, as is fitting in the Lord. Husbands, love your wives and do not be embittered against them. Children, be obedient to your parents in all things, for this is well-pleasing to the Lord. Fathers, do not exasperate your children, so that they will not lose heart. *Colossians 3:18–21 (NASB)*

He who spares the rod hates his son, but he who loves him is careful to discipline him. *Proverbs 13:24*

Do not withhold discipline from a child; if you punish him with the rod, he will not die. Punish him with the rod and save his soul from death. [Hades] *Proverbs 23: 13–14*

Discipline your son, for in that there is hope; do not be a willing party to his death. *Proverbs 19:18*

He who ignores discipline despises himself, but whoever heeds correction gains understanding. *Proverbs 15:32*

A wise son brings joy to his father, but a foolish son grief to his mother. *Proverbs 10:1*

Honor your father and mother as the LORD your God has commanded you, so that you may live long and that it may go well with you in the land the LORD your God is giving you. *Deuteronomy 5:16*

Children, obey your parents in the Lord, for this is right. Honor your father and mother (which is the first commandment with a promise), so that it may be well with you, and that you may live long on the earth. Fathers, do not provoke your children to anger, but bring them up in the discipline and instruction of the Lord. *Ephesians 6:1–4 (NASB)*

Advice on parenting from Jesus: After an argument with my teenage son, I was awakened to Jesus saying to me, "If you love me, you will obey me." Right away I responded, "He is not honoring and obeying his parents." Jesus answered, "You are not obeying my greatest command." Instantly, "love" came to mind. "Ohhh…

ouch," I thought. Arguing with Jesus is pointless. Since learning this, I can see when the devil is coming at me with condemnation that my children are not as obedient as they should be and I am reminded that love covers a multitude of sins. God teaches us how we should praise and affirm our love to our children when He proclaims, "This is my Son, whom I love; with him I am well pleased." (Matthew 3:17) Make sure you are building your child's confidence up by praising what they do well. I always held back praises from my children to prevent them from getting a big head. I was wrong. They desire and need our affirmations.

[Jesus said] Love one another, as I have loved you. John 15:12
"Let all that you do be done in love." 1 Corinthians 6:14 (NJKV)

Surviving teenagers is a monumental task. Worldliness, rebellion, and a lack of respect can easily take hold. If this has happened in your family, pray that Jesus changes their heart back to Him. Give them over into God's loving hands and lay them upon His altar. They are not yours, but His. God will take over for He alone knows their needs and what it will take to break their rebellion. God will bring circumstances into their lives that bring them to His truth. God will also give us, as parents, the wisdom and love to guide them back to His truth. A good summer Bible camp can be the perfect way to reignite the flame. *LORD, please give us strength, wisdom, and love through these years.*

Fathers are instructed to teach their children in the ways of the LORD. Reading the Book of Proverbs allows children to receive God's wisdom of how to live a godly life. For your older children, the Book of James and 1 John get right to the point of how to apply the Word of God in their lives. As head of the household, the father is also the disciplinarian. The Bible instructs a father to discipline his children **because** he loves them and not to break their spirit. Create a contract with your child that sets boundaries and establishes rewards. Our heavenly Father loves us unconditionally and He disciplines us out of love because He wants what is best for us. Children should fear consequences for bad behavior because on the Day of Judgment there will be consequences for our sins if we have not repented.

God has brought my husband to the point where he knows that he is not supposed to just be a friend to our children but have the authority needed for them to know he means business. He even asked them for forgiveness for not being the father he was supposed to be. What a man! The fighting between my husband and I has virtually stopped (unless, of course, I fall back into my ways of controlling or our children try to manipulate us.) I have less stress now because all I have to say is that the behavior had better stop or they will have to deal with their father. I can now concentrate on my part of being nurturing and loving, and not a nag. Your husband will get much more attractive as well.

The best thing that we as mothers can do in the morning for our children is to pray daily for their individual needs, pray for their school, for their future spouse, and put the armor of God on them. My family is <u>very</u> dysfunctional if we do not follow the rules listed above. God made the rules and we all have to play by them to be successful. When we as Christians obey what God commands, the family dynamics will be healthier than ever before. Satan will lose his foothold of breaking down our families.

> *Praise the LORD! Blessed is the man who fears the LORD, Who delights greatly in His commandments. His descendants will be mighty on earth; The generation of the upright will be blessed. Psalm 112:1–2 (NKJV)*

A Father's Simple Prayer

I love you, (child's name). Jesus loves you. Serve Him with humility and kindness to others. This can only come through strength; His strength in you.

A Daily Prayer for your Child's School

Heavenly Father, I plead the blood of Jesus over (school's name) as an umbrella of protection. I claim the power of the light of Jesus to be present in every classroom, hallway, and office. Where Jesus' light is, there can be no darkness. I ask You, Jesus, to send down mighty angels to protect the doors so that no evil may enter and only good dwells within. I ask for spiritual wisdom and revelation for the teachers and administration and that the peace of the Lord be upon them and all of the children. I claim Jesus' victory over this school and everyone within. In Jesus' name I pray, amen.

If you are a single mom or dad, our prayer is that God will grant you mercy and wisdom to be able to fulfill both roles for your children and that God will provide the godly people in their lives to fulfill all their needs. Psalm 68:5 tells us that God is the "Father to the fatherless".

Journaling Exercise

1. Read Proverbs 31 for the instructions of "A Wife of Noble Character" and Psalm 1 for a righteous husband and take notes of their character.

2. Listen online with your children/teenagers to the country song by Tim McGraw, "Humble and Kind."

3. What can you do to get your family life in order? List some goals.

Helpful Suggestions: If your baby or small child has trouble sleeping, purchase "Lullabies for Lil' Lambs" by Whispering Angels. This cd works every time. A great reference book for parents is "Against the Grain: Raising Christ-Focused Children from A to Z" by Dr. Michelle White.

WEEK 9
GROUP QUESTIONS

1. What are some of the quality traits of someone with a servant's heart?

2. Did God reveal to anyone what He would like you to do with your time, talent, and/or treasure?

3. Do you have a stronghold in your marriage? Pray for each other for God to mend these strongholds.

4. How have you been able to show respect/love to your mate?

5. Read out loud Proverbs 31 for the instructions of "A Wife of Noble Character" and Psalm 1 for a righteous husband. Discuss the traits for each.

6. Have you started implementing new rules in your household for your children? If so, tell how they are working.

7. Lift up the needs of your children in prayer. Give them over to God to work in them.

Week 10

LIVING AN ABUNDANT
LIFE IN CHRIST

This is my comfort in my affliction, that your promise gives me life.
Psalm 119:50 (ESV)

Lesson 36
SUFFERING

*I*n our lives, there will be periods of suffering. Sometimes it will be physical or mental, other times by persecution of our faith, or by the actions of others. When Paul pleaded to the LORD to take away the thorn in his flesh given to him by the devil, he was told that the LORD'S power is made perfect in weakness. It is in our suffering that we receive God's best because we rely completely on Him as He teaches us.

Amongst our pain and suffering, we seem to have to grapple with sin. This sin is in our lives as a result of what we caused or what was done to us. We can be healed and grow by persevering through life's difficulties. The Bible reveals that as we suffer in the body, we die to sin. We must all come to the heart of sin and meet Jesus. In my life I had to forgive and let pain go as well as repent of sin.

The verse where James writes "count it all joy" whenever we face trials is a very difficult pill to swallow in times of suffering (James 1:2). Romans 8:28 tells us that "in all things God works for the good of those who love him, who have been called according to his purpose." It is hard to consider any joy or good that comes out of our suffering. The very next line (Romans 8:29) reveals that "for those God foreknew he also predestined to be conformed to the likeness of his Son." As we suffer, we are being conformed, made to grow, into the image of Christ. Like an oyster that suffers from embedded sand, this suffering produces a beautiful pearl.

Heavenly Father, I pray that You will speak to me through Your Word and provide divine understanding of Your truth. Give me ears to hear and eyes to see and a heart to understand. In Jesus' name I pray, amen.

[Paul said] Because of the surpassing greatness of the revelations, for this reason, to keep me from exalting myself, there was given me a thorn in the flesh, a messenger of Satan to torment me—to keep me from exalting myself! Concerning this I implored the Lord three times that it might leave me. And He has said to me, "My grace is sufficient for you, for power is perfected in weakness." Most gladly, therefore, I will rather boast about my weaknesses, so that the power of Christ may dwell in me. Therefore I am well content with weaknesses, with insults, with distresses, with persecutions, with difficulties, for Christ's sake; for when I am weak, then I am strong. *2 Corinthians 12:7–10 (NASB)*

Therefore, since Christ suffered in his body, arm yourselves also with the same attitude, because he who has suffered in his body is done with sin. As a result, he does not live the rest of his earthly life for evil human desires, but rather for the will of God. *1 Peter 4:1–2*

Not only so, but we also rejoice in our sufferings, because we know that suffering produces perseverance; perseverance, character; and character, hope. And hope does not disappoint us, because God has poured out his love into our hearts by the Holy Spirit, whom he has given us. *Romans 5:3–5*

The Bible tells us that we must share in Jesus' suffering in order to experience His resurrection power. In other words, we must die to ourselves through our sufferings so that we may live for Christ and produce fruit. Whatever the desperate trials we must go through cannot compare to what we gain in truly knowing and living for Jesus.

Yet indeed I also count all things loss for the excellence of the knowledge of Christ Jesus my Lord, for whom I have suffered the loss of all things, and count them as rubbish, that I may gain Christ and be found in

Him, not having my own righteousness, which is from the law, but that which is through faith in Christ, the righteousness which is from God by faith: that I may know Him and the power of His resurrection, and the fellowship of His sufferings, being conformed to His death, if, by any means, I may attain to the resurrection from the dead. Philippians 3:8–10 (NKJV)

[Jesus said] Truly, truly I say to you, unless a grain of wheat falls into the earth and dies, it remains alone; but if it dies, it bears much fruit. John 12:24 (ESV)

There are many reasons God allows us to suffer. In the case of Job, he was righteous, and God allowed him to suffer. Christians benefit by seeing Job's faithfulness during his intense suffering and also that he was rewarded for persevering. Paul suffered and was given great revelations through his trials. In all trials, God is in control, and we must seek His strength and love. Fully submit your illness or trial to God and His will for the outcome. As described in Psalm 84, we will go through periods of "baca", which translates as "weeping," knowing that we have the hope that we will be strengthened, convicted, and renewed by the Holy Spirit (the springs), and the coming of Jesus (the autumn rains). We are called to take up our cross daily, persevere, praise God in this storm, and seek Him in everything.

Brothers, as an example of patience in the face of suffering, take the prophets who spoke in the name of the Lord. As you know, we consider blessed those who have persevered. You have heard of Job's perseverance and have seen what the Lord finally brought about. The Lord is full of compassion and mercy. James 5:10–11

Blessed are those whose strength is in you, who have set their hearts on pilgrimage. As they pass through the Valley of Baca, they make it a place of springs; the autumn rains also cover it with pools. They go from strength to strength till each appears before God in Zion. Psalm 84:6–7

Be self-controlled and alert. Your enemy the devil prowls around like a roaring lion looking for someone to devour. Resist him, standing firm in the faith, because you know that your brothers throughout the world are undergoing the same kind of sufferings. And the God of all grace, who called you to his eternal glory in Christ, after you have suffered a little while, will himself restore you and make you strong, firm and steadfast. 1Peter 5:8–10

During our suffering we get to see a glimpse of the glory to come when we will be able to walk with Him and talk with Him and share in the bounty of Heaven. Charles Spurgeon writes in "Morning by Morning", "Therefore, thank God if your road has been rough, for this is what has given you the experience of God's greatness and loving-kindness. Our troubles have enriched you with a wealth of knowledge not gained in any other way, for your trials have been the "cleft in the rock" where Jehovah has put you, just as he did with His servant Moses, that you might behold His Glory as it "passes by". (Exodus 33:22)

The Spirit himself testifies with our spirit that we are God's children. Now if we are children, then we are heirs-heirs of God and co-heirs with Christ if indeed we share in his sufferings in order that we may also share in his glory. I consider that our present sufferings are not worth comparing with the glory that will be revealed in us. Romans 8:16–18

Why we suffer is different for everyone and we should not judge each other like the three "friends" of Job. One friend blamed Job's suffering on him being evil, one blamed him for being wicked and sinful, and one blamed him of being uncharitable and questioning God's authority. All three of them were wrong and they were severely chastened by God. One thing is for sure, evil exists in this world and will try to harm us. We need to lift each other up in prayer and fight for one another.

If you know someone who has suffered a great loss, the very best thing you can do is mourn with them. I have a friend who lost her 29-year-old daughter who deeply loved the Lord and suffered from seizures. (Her photo is in Lesson 30.) During the first year after her death, we shed many tears together. It is not the time to reason why it happened but to walk alongside of them. Pray for God to reveal answers in His timing. God did reveal scripture to comfort her. (2 Timothy 4:6–8 and Isaiah 57:1–2)

We must ask Jesus to heal us of our infirmities. Miracles still occur. The woman who bled for 12 years knew in faith that she had only to touch the clothes of Jesus to be healed. The blind beggar knew that if he asked Jesus to heal him, he would be healed. We must ask in faith that at any point, Jesus can heal us. Praise God during this period for the hope that we have from His Son of our eternal salvation. Especially while in the fire, rejoice that our Savior and Lord is in control and some day we will meet Him face to face.

When she heard about Jesus, she came behind Him in the crowd and touched His garment. For she said, "If only I may touch His clothes, I shall be made well." Immediately the fountain of her blood was dried up, and she felt in her body that she was healed of the affliction. And Jesus, immediately knowing in Himself that power had gone out of Him, turned around in the crowd and said, "Who touched My clothes?" ... But the woman, fearing and trembling, knowing what had happened to her, came and fell down before Him and told Him the whole truth. And He said to her, "Daughter, your faith has made you well. Go in peace, and be healed of your affliction." Mark 5:27–30 & Mark 5:33–34 (NKJV)

Then those who went before warned him that he should be quiet; but he cried out all the more, "Son of David, have mercy on me!" So Jesus stood still and commanded him to be brought to Him. And when he had come near, He asked him, saying, "What do you want Me to do for you?" He said, "Lord, that I may receive my sight." Then Jesus said to him, "Receive your sight; your faith has made you well." And immediately he received his sight, and followed Him, glorifying God. And all the people, when they saw it, gave praise to God. Luke 18:39–43 (NKJV)

You may need to pray that the spirit of infirmity be lifted from you or a loved one in Jesus' name. You can command that "by His stripes you are healed." The Bible instructs those who are sick to go to your church and have the elders pray over you and anoint your head with oil in the name of the Lord. If needed, confess your sins to a trusted Christian sister or brother and make what is hidden, revealed. James 5 says to confess your sins, pray for each other and be healed. The blood of Jesus washes away all sin and the 'prayer of a righteous man availeth much.'

> *Surely he hath borne our griefs, and carried our sorrows, yet we did not esteem him stricken, smitten of God, and afflicted. But he was wounded for our transgressions, he was bruised for our iniquities: the chastisement of our peace was upon him; and with his stripes we are healed. Isaiah 53:4–5 (KJV)*
>
> *Is any one of you sick? He should call the elders of the church to pray over him and anoint him with oil in the name of the Lord. And the prayer offered in faith will make the sick person well; the Lord will raise him up. If he has sinned, he will be forgiven. Therefore confess your sins to each other and pray for each other so that you may be healed. The prayer of a righteous man is powerful and effective. James 5:14–16*

Testimony of Healing by Jerrilea (my mother-in-law)

I accepted the Lord in 1974, but I did not believe in miracles. In 1984, I was diagnosed with a cancerous tumor that wrapped around the optic nerve of my right eye. The first radiation treatment did not work. By the summer of 1985, the tumor had grown to about two inches and I was no longer able to see out of that eye and was having severe headaches.

When I became too ill to work, my Christian friends took turns coming over to clean and care for my two younger children. These ladies would lay hands on me and pray for me and tell me that I was going to be healed. I did not have faith that this would happen. One of the ladies took me to her church to a "Miracle Service." The pastor laid hands on me and I woke up on the floor. Everyone that had been praying for me there told me that I was healed. I didn't believe them and went to my scheduled surgery five days later. When the surgeon cut me open, the tumor was the size of a pea. He had it biopsied and it came back as now benign. Six weeks later I got my eyesight back. Jesus healed me through the faith of others!

Example of a Prayer for Healing Sickness (lay hands on the area of pain)
*Heavenly Father, we praise You and thank you for Your great love and mercy. Lord Jesus, You are Emmanuel, God with us, and You comfort us and heal us. When You walked this earth You healed the sick of their afflictions, and You still do. The woman who bled for 12 years knew if she just touched Your garment then she would be healed. We ask to touch the tassels of Your garment and be healed. By her faith she was healed. The blind beggar asked for mercy and to be healed of his blindness. By his faith You healed him. We stand firm in our faith and we <u>ask</u> You, Jesus, son of David, for Your mercy and for _____ to be miraculously healed. You said that this sign shall accompany those who believe, that they can "place their hands on sick people, and they will get well." In the name of Jesus Christ, **be healed**. We ask to loose this spirit of infirmity. Loose any sorrow, illness, and pain that is not from You, and bind it to the healing love from You, Jesus.*

In Deuteronomy it is written that the diseases of Egypt shall not touch Your people and in Revelation it is written that the enemy was overcome by the blood of the Lamb. In the name of Jesus Christ of Nazareth, we claim Your resurrection power and Your blood poured over_____ to overcome this illness and by Your stripes they are healed.

May the will of our Father be done and the peace of the LORD be upon _____. In Jesus' precious name we pray, amen.

Keep your hands on the area of pain and praise and thank God.

*"**Holy, holy, holy is the Lord God Almighty, who was, and is, and is to come.**" Revelation 4:8b*

Journaling Exercise
1. Please listen to the song online by The City Harmonic from Heart, "Love, Heal Me" and reflect on this beautiful, healing song. Next listen to "Healer" by Jesus Culture and praise Him.

2. If you are in the "eye of the storm" of your suffering then listen online to "Eye of the Storm" by Ryan Stevenson.

3. If you are about to go into a surgery, read Psalm 23. I memorized and recited it while being wheeled in and received so much comfort in His promise. If it is in regards to your heart, pray that God guards your heart, for it is the wellspring of life. God is in control and has you in the palm of His hand.

4. Write down a prayer to Jesus for healing of yourself or someone you know.

Be still, and know that I am God. I will be exalted
among the nations, I will be exalted in the earth!
Psalm 46:10 (ESV)

Lesson 37

PERSECUTION

ecause we follow Jesus, we will face persecution. The Bible guarantees it. We are instructed to take up our cross daily and persevere. People, even those we love, will at some point come against us with the desire to harm us because we follow Jesus. We must choose Jesus first above all other relationships. Being attacked in the workplace is very common. During these trials we will definitely grow; especially in humility and learning to place our full trust in God. Keep in perspective the persecution that we are going through and the stark comparison to the persecution that Jesus endured.

Heavenly Father, I pray that You will speak to me through Your Word and provide divine understanding of Your truth. Give me ears to hear and eyes to see and a heart to understand. In Jesus' name I pray, amen.

In fact, everyone who wants to live a godly life in Christ Jesus will be persecuted. *2 Timothy 3:12*

"Do not think that I came to bring peace on the earth; I did not come to bring peace, but a sword. For I came to set a man against his father, and a daughter against her mother, and a daughter-in-law against her mother-in-law; and a man's enemies will be the members of his household. He who loves father or mother more than Me is not worthy of Me; and he who loves son or daughter more than Me is not

worthy of Me. And he who does not take his cross and follow after Me is not worthy of Me." Matthew 10:34–38 (NASB)

Blessed are those who are persecuted because of righteousness, for theirs is the kingdom of heaven. Blessed are you when people insult you, persecute you and falsely say all kinds of evil against you because of me. Rejoice and be glad, because great is your reward in heaven, for in the same way they persecuted the prophets who were before you. Matthew 5:10–12

But how is it to your credit if you receive a beating for doing wrong and endure it? But if you suffer for doing good and you endure it, this is commendable before God. To this you were called, because Christ suffered for you, leaving you an example that you should follow in his steps. 1Peter 2: 20–21

Trust in the LORD that He will bring us through these times of trial. Seek His refuge. Psalm 91, verse 1, tells us that "He who dwells in the shelter of the Most High will rest in the shadow of the Almighty." God will renew our strength as we place our hope in Him. Stand firm. Because we have chosen His refuge, He will protect us, shelter us, and see us through.

From my distress I called upon the LORD; the LORD answered me and set me in a large place. The LORD is for me; I will not fear; What can man do to me? The LORD is for me among those who help me; therefore I will look with satisfaction on those who hate me. It is better to take refuge in the LORD than to trust in man. It is better to take refuge in the LORD than to trust in princes. All nations surrounded me; in the name of the LORD I will surely cut them off. They surrounded me, yes, they surrounded me; in the name of the LORD I will surely cut them off. Psalm 118:5–11 (NASB)

Even youths grow tired and weary, and young men stumble and fall; but those who hope in the LORD will renew their strength. They will soar on wings like eagles; they will run and not grow weary, they will walk and not be faint. Isaiah 40:30–31

It is well with the man who deals generously and lends; who conducts his affairs with justice. For the righteous will never be moved; he will be remembered forever. He is not afraid of bad news; his heart is firm, trusting in the LORD. His heart is steady; he will not be afraid, until he looks in triumph on his adversaries. Psalm 112:5–8 (ESV)

Teach me Your way, O LORD, and lead me in a level path because of my foes. Do not deliver me over to the desire of my adversaries, for false witnesses have risen against me, and such as breathe out violence. I would have despaired unless I had believed that I would see the goodness of the LORD in the land of the living. Wait for the LORD; be strong and let your heart take courage; yes, wait for the LORD. Psalm 27:11–14 (NASB)

"Do not touch My anointed ones, And do My prophets no harm." Psalm 105:15 (NASB)

"Because you have made the Lord your refuge, and the Most High your dwelling place, there shall no evil befall you, nor any plague or calamity come near your tent. For He will give his angels [especial] charge (directions, instructions) over you to accompany, and defend and preserve you in all your ways [of obedience and service]." Psalm 91:9–11 (AMPC)

Cast your burden upon the LORD and He will sustain you; He will never allow the righteous to be shaken. Psalm 55:22 (NASB)

Because of the LORD'S great love we are not consumed, for his compassions never fail. They are new every morning; great is your faithfulness. Lamentations 3:22–23

Prayer for Persecution (Substitute name, he/she and him/her)

Heavenly Father, we praise You for Your loving kindness and we ask that we can come before You and lift _____ to Your throne and that You grant Your great mercy. _____ has suffered for doing good and, as it is written, this is commendable to the Lord. Those who wish to harm _____ surround _____, and we ask that, like Daniel, the mouths of these lions are shut. We stand firm in our faith and claim Your words that 'no weapon that is formed against _____ shall prosper and every tongue that accuses_____ in judgment You will condemn'. This is our heritage that You promise.

God we know that You hate injustice and iniquity. We ask for Your justice to prevail. You say in 1 Chronicles, "Beware, lest you touch my anointed," and in Deuteronomy You tell us that "It is mine to avenge; I will repay." Thank you for these promises.

Please grant favor to _____ in the eyes of those that oppose_____. We claim Your promise that those of Yours that have been shamed or disgraced shall inherit a double portion. We rejoice that You tell us that "If God is for you, who can be against you!" And that "The LORD is with me; I will not be afraid, what can man do to me?"

We trust you, LORD, and we give You this battle, for as it is written, 'the battle is the Lord's'. We commit this situation to You. Lead us to victory.

In Lamentations it is written: "Because of the LORD'S great love we are not consumed, for his compassions never fail. They are new every morning; great is your faithfulness."

Thank you, Father, for great is Your faithfulness. In Your Almighty Son's name we pray, amen.

Lay whatever is burdening you on God's altar; everything belongs to Him. If there is any idol that you have not surrendered to God, give it over to Him. God says He is a jealous God and will tear down any idol in our life. If it is a fear of not being provided for, surrender it to God. If it is pride, give it over to Him. If your work is an idol, lay it at His altar. Surrender your job to Him, and know that He gave you the job and will either see you through until you prosper, or give you something better. Praise God while in the fire.

God places everyone in authority over us. We are sometimes given situations where we are persecuted to grow us more into the image of Jesus. Remember that Jesus was a humble servant that was born in a manger and came in on a donkey. He washed the feet of His disciples to show us how we are to act. Unless the action goes against the authority of God, we are to give reverence and loyalty to those in authority over us.

Sometimes it is necessary to make an appeal, or petition, to those in authority over you. A great reference on the web can be found when you type in "How can I make an effective appeal? Institute in Basic Life Principles." This outlines how to give a godly appeal that is biblically-based.

When my husband and I were going through a long period of persecution, while in prayer, the Holy Spirit spoke to me the below passage in Philippians. This passage has become the answer for us to any difficult situation.

Do not be anxious for anything, but in everything, by prayer and petition, with thanksgiving, present your requests to God. And the peace of God, which transcends all understanding, will guard your hearts and your minds in Christ Jesus. Philippians 4:6–7

Jesus instructs us to love our enemies. Pray for them to find salvation and to truly know Jesus. God will honor your prayers. After this period of persecution came to an end, my husband and I (slowly) learned to forgive them and give it over to Jesus, be thankful of past provision, and take comfort that God is in control of our future. The battle is the LORD'S. Praise God in advance for what He is going to do for you.

But I tell you: Love your enemies and pray for those who persecute you, that you may be sons of your Father in heaven. Matthew 5:44–45a
    But you will not leave in haste or go in flight; for the LORD will go before you, the God of Israel will be your rear guard. Isaiah 52:12

Journaling Exercise

1. Please listen online to "God Will Take Care of You – Hymn" by Run With Endurance. Practice lying or kneeling down and closing your eyes and feeling Jesus' embrace around you and tell Him what's burdening you. Jot down your experience.

Pray for the peace of Jerusalem, they shall prosper that love thee.
Psalm 122:6 (KJV)

Lesson 38

TIES TO ISRAEL

The Israelites are the first chosen people of God. They are the branches of the olive tree that represent God's people. The olive tree's roots consist of Abraham, Isaac, and Jacob and Jesus came in the form of a man from this bloodline. God gave the land of Israel to Abraham and the descendants of Isaac and Jacob. Israel is referred to as the holy root in Romans 11 and Jesus is the source of the root. Jesus tells us that "I am the Root and the Offspring of David, and the bright Morning Star." (Revelation 22:16)

In Romans 11 we learn that because of the Israelites' transgressions and disobedience, God allowed us Gentiles that have faith in His Son to be grafted into this olive tree to make Israel envious. Due to their unbelief, some of the Jewish branches were broken off, and now we are grafted in and share from the same sap of the olive root. Abraham is now our father too. We must not look down upon our Jewish brothers but understand that we are grafted in because of them, and can be cut out as well.

Heavenly Father, I pray that You will speak to me through Your Word and provide divine understanding of Your truth. Give me ears to hear and eyes to see and a heart to understand. In Jesus' name I pray, amen.

For if the first fruit is holy, the lump is also holy; and if the root is holy, so are the branches. And if some of the branches were broken off, and you, being a wild olive tree, were grafted in among them, and with

them became a partaker of the root and fatness of the olive tree, do not boast against the branches. But if you do boast, remember that you do not support the root, but the root supports you. You will say then, "Branches were broken off that I might be grafted in." Well said. Because of unbelief they were broken off, and you stand by faith. Do not be haughty, but fear. For if God did not spare the natural branches, He may not spare you either. Therefore consider the goodness and severity of God: on those who fell, severity; but toward you, goodness, if you continue in His goodness. Otherwise you also will be cut off.
Romans 11:16–22 (NKJV)

We will soon be a part of the "new man" that combines Jews and Gentiles by the blood of Jesus. We are citizens of the New Jerusalem. Our fate has an integral part in Israel and His first chosen people. We are to pray for Israel and bring the good news to them by showing kindness and loyal support.

I will bless those who bless you, and whoever curses you I will curse; and all peoples on earth will be blessed through you. Genesis 12:3

Therefore remember that formerly you, the Gentiles in the flesh, who are called "Uncircumcision" by the so-called "Circumcision," which is performed in the flesh by human hands— remember that you were at that time separate from Christ, excluded from the commonwealth of Israel, and strangers to the covenants of promise, having no hope and without God in the world. But now in Christ Jesus you who formerly were far off have been brought near by the blood of Christ. For He Himself is our peace, who made both groups into one and broke down the barrier of the dividing wall, by abolishing in His flesh the enmity, which is the Law of commandments contained in ordinances, so that in Himself He might make the two into one new man, thus establishing peace, and might reconcile them both in one body to God through the cross, by it having put to death the enmity. Ephesians 2:11–16 (NASB)

Brethren, my heart's desire and prayer to God for Israel is that they may be saved. For I bear them witness that they have a zeal for

God, but not according to knowledge. For they being ignorant of God's righteousness, and seeking to establish their own righteousness, have not submitted to the righteousness of God. For Christ is the end of the law for righteousness to everyone who believes. Romans 10:1–4 (NKJV)

For there is no distinction between Jew and Greek, for the same Lord over all is rich to all who call upon Him. For "whoever calls on the name of the LORD shall be saved." Romans 10:12–13 (NKJV)

Israel is very important to God, as it should be to us as Christians. Pray for the peace of Israel in your daily prayers. This holy nation is where Jesus will return.

I will bring back my exiled people Israel; they will rebuild the ruined cities and live in them. They will plant vineyards and drink their wine; they will make gardens and eat their fruit. I will plant Israel in their own land, never again to be uprooted from the land I have given them," says the LORD your God. Amos 9:14–15

Pray for the peace of Jerusalem: "May they prosper who love you. Peace be within your walls, prosperity within your palaces." For the sake of my brethren and companions, I will now say, "Peace be within you." Because of the house of the LORD our God I will seek your good. Psalm 122:6–9 (NKJV)

Pass through, pass through the gates! Prepare the way for the people. Build up, build up the highway! Remove the stones. Raise a banner for the nations. The LORD has made proclamation to the ends of the earth: "Say to the Daughter of Zion, See, your Savior comes! See, his reward is with him, and his recompense accompanies him." Isaiah 62:10–11

Journaling Exercise

1. Pray and ask God to reveal His thoughts about Israel to you.

Lift up your heads, O you gates! And be lifted up,
O ancient doors, that the King of glory may come in.
Psalm 24:7(ESV)

Lesson 39

COME, LORD JESUS

*I*t is important for us to know how Jesus will come back to us so that we will be ready. We must keep watch for Him and advise others how He will return so that they are not deceived by false christs. Knowing that His return is imminent inspires us to try to help others learn the truth so that they too will be taken up with Jesus.

[Jesus said] For false christs and false prophets will rise and show great signs and wonders to deceive, if possible, even the elect. See, I have told you beforehand. "Therefore if they say to you, 'Look, He is in the desert!' do not go out; or 'Look, He is in the inner rooms!' do not believe it. For as the lightning comes from the east and flashes to the west, so also will the coming of the Son of Man be. Matthew 24:24–27 (NKJV)

For the Lord Himself will descend from heaven with a shout, with the voice of an archangel, and with the trumpet of God. And the dead in Christ will rise first. Then we who are alive and remain shall be caught up together with them in the clouds to meet the Lord in the air. And thus we shall always be with the Lord. Therefore comfort one another with these words. 1 Thessalonians 4:16–18 (NKJV)

[Jesus said] "But know this, that if the master of the house had known what hour the thief would come, he would have watched and not allowed his house to be broken into. Therefore you also be

ready, for the Son of Man is coming at an hour you do not expect."
Luke 12:39–40 (NKJV)

As we get closer to the Day of the Lord, God promises to pour out His Spirit in an even greater way so we can hear Him. Expect to hear from Him. Enter into His rest with joy. Seek His will in everything and offer yourself to Him to do His work.

"And it shall come to pass afterward, that I will pour out my spirit upon all flesh: and your sons and your daughters shall prophesy, your old men shall dream dreams, your young men shall see visions: And also upon the servants and upon the handmaids in those days will I pour out my spirit. And I will show wonders in the heavens and in the earth, blood, and fire, and pillars of smoke. The sun shall be turned into darkness, and the moon into blood, before the great and the terrible day of the LORD come. And it shall come to pass, that whosoever shall call on the name of the LORD shall be delivered: for in mount Zion and in Jerusalem shall be deliverance, as the LORD hath said, and in the remnant whom the LORD shall call." Joel 2:28–32 (KJV)

The Bible instructs us of the signs of the End of the Age. Jesus revealed that "nation will rise against nation, and kingdom against kingdom. There will be great earthquakes, famines and pestilences in various places, and fearful events and great signs from heaven." (Luke 22:10–11) There will be signs in the sun, moon, and stars. The sun will turn to darkness, the moon to blood, and the stars will fall. The Bible also tells us that Elijah will be sent to us before the Day of the Lord.

The sun shall be turned into darkness, and the moon into blood, before the coming of the great and awesome day of the Lord. And it shall come to pass That whoever calls on the name of the Lord Shall be saved. Acts 2:20–21 (NKJV)

[Jesus said] "Immediately after the tribulation of those days the sun will be darkened, and the moon will not give its light; the stars will fall from heaven, and the powers of the heavens will be shaken. Then the

sign of the Son of Man will appear in heaven, and then all the tribes of the earth will mourn, and they will see the Son of Man coming on the clouds of heaven with power and great glory. And He will send His angels with a great sound of a trumpet, and they will gather together His elect from the four winds, from one end of heaven to the other." Matthew 24:29–31 (NKJV)

Jesus answered and said to them, "Indeed, Elijah is coming first and will restore all things." Matthew 17:11 (NKJV)

Behold, I will send you Elijah the prophet before the coming of the great and dreadful day of the LORD. Malachi 4:5 (NKJV)

2 Thessalonians 2 (Man of Lawlessness) tells us that this man of lawlessness must be revealed before the coming of Jesus. Read this chapter to be aware of this man and how Jesus will eliminate him. We are instructed to stand firm and know that we are saved. Our hope is found in the promise of Jesus' imminent return.

"In my vision at night I looked, and there before me was one like a son of man, coming with the clouds of heaven. He approached the Ancient of Days and was led into his presence. He was given authority, glory and sovereign power; all peoples, nations and men of every language worshiped him. His dominion is an everlasting dominion that will not pass away, and his kingdom is one that will never be destroyed." Daniel 7:13–14

I saw the Holy City, the new Jerusalem, coming down out of heaven from God, prepared as a bride beautifully dressed for her husband. And I heard a loud voice from the throne saying, "Now the dwelling of God is with men, and he will live with them. They will be his people, and God himself will be with them and be their God. He will wipe away every tear from their eyes. There will be no more death or mourning or crying or pain, for the old order of things has passed away." Revelation 21:2–4

Let us rejoice and be glad and give him glory! For the wedding of the Lamb has come, and his bride has made herself ready. Fine linen, bright and clean, was given her to wear." (Fine Linen stands for the righteous acts of the saints.) Then the angel said to me, "Write: 'Blessed are those who are invited to the wedding supper of the Lamb!'" And he added, "These are the true words of God." Revelation 19:7–9

He who testifies to these things says, "Yes, I am coming soon." Amen. Come, Lord Jesus. Revelation 22:20

Journaling Exercise

1. Please read Mathew 24, Mark 13, and Luke 22 for more instructions from Jesus concerning His return. Take notes to compare the similarities in each book.

2. Please listen online to "Even So Come" by Kristian Stanfill and then "Holy" (Wedding Day) by City Harmonic. This second song tells of the New Jerusalem and the Wedding Supper of the Lamb. The church is His bride and He is the bridegroom.

Sing praises to the LORD, who dwells in Zion!
Declare His deeds among the people.
Psalm 9:11 (NKJV)

Lesson 40
INCREASE HIS KINGDOM

W hy has Jesus not returned yet? Because God is building His Kingdom, and He wants us to make His numbers increase so that multitudes around the world and within our neighborhoods are saved and will know Jesus when He comes, and His bride, the Church, will be waiting for Him.

Since 1999 God has been showing me the number 911 two times in a row. I was not yet a Christian, but I would see this number in a variety of circumstances. At first I would panic and think that something terrible was about to happen. Slowly I came to realize that it meant that He was warning me to pay attention: I was going to learn something.

Right after I accepted the Lord, I began putting this book together as a way to understand what I was learning and not forget. Almost every week I would see 911 twice in a row and was open to what I was about to learn when I saw these numbers. Many times, He would show me a verse in the Bible or speak a verse throughout the night and then I would go to church or a Bible study and the topic would be on that very thing. It was very common within the same week to get the same message three different ways.

When I chose the psalm for this lesson, for some reason it didn't register that the verse was 9:11. Two years later, it dawned on me; this was His ultimate message all along, to increase His Kingdom. We must snatch people from the fire and know that it was not long ago that we were as deceived by the world as they are.

Heavenly Father, I pray that You will speak to me through Your Word and provide divine understanding of Your truth. Give me ears to hear and eyes to see and a heart to understand. In Jesus' name I pray, amen.

Until we all reach unity in the faith and in the knowledge of the Son of God and become mature, attaining the whole measure of the fullness of Christ. *Ephesians 4:13*

Then Jesus said to His disciples, "If anyone wishes to come after Me, he must deny himself, and take up his cross and follow Me. For whoever wishes to save his life will lose it; but whoever loses his life for My sake will find it. *Matthew 16:24–25 (NASB)*

But you, beloved, building yourselves up on your most holy faith, praying in the Holy Spirit, keep yourselves in the love of God, waiting anxiously for the mercy of our Lord Jesus Christ to eternal life. And have mercy on some, who are doubting; save others, snatching them out of the fire; and on some have mercy with fear, hating even the garment polluted by the flesh. *Jude 1:20–23 (NASB)*

Walk in wisdom toward outsiders, making the best use of the time. Let your speech always be gracious, seasoned with salt, so that you may know how you ought to answer each person. *Colossians 4:5–6 (ESV)*

For we also once were foolish ourselves, disobedient, deceived, enslaved to various lusts and pleasures, spending our life in malice and envy, hateful, hating one another. But when the kindness of God our Savior and His love for mankind appeared, He saved us, not on the basis of deeds which we have done in righteousness, but according to His mercy, by the washing of regeneration and renewing by the Holy Spirit, whom He poured out upon us richly through Jesus Christ our Savior, so that being justified by His grace we would be made heirs according to the hope of eternal life. *Titus 3:3–7 (NASB)*

The end of all things is near; therefore, be of sound judgment and sober spirit for the purpose of prayer. Above all, keep fervent in your love for one another, because love covers a multitude of sins. Be hospitable to one another without complaint. As each one has received a special

gift, employ it in serving one another as good stewards of the manifold grace of God. Whoever speaks, is to do so as one who is speaking the utterances of God; whoever serves is to do so as one who is serving by the strength which God supplies; so that in all things God may be glorified through Jesus Christ, to whom belongs the glory and dominion forever and ever. Amen. 1 Peter 4: 7–11 (NASB)

Living an Abundant Life in Christ

How can we attain an abundant life in Christ to help us fill His Kingdom? The answer is just as much for me, the author, as the reader to put into daily practice. How easy it is to forget, get distracted, or discouraged from the race and the prize that awaits us.

We live our life abundantly when we have a contrite heart of knowing how sinful we are yet living "in full assurance of faith" (Hebrews 10:22) that our glorious standing with God comes from Jesus Christ. God sees His righteous Son when He looks at us. We live our life abundantly when we delight in the Father and His unconditional love for us. Knowing these two things deep in our spirit makes us love and want to please Him even more. May we desire to be holy and full of His grace.

> *Therefore, preparing your minds for action, and being sober-minded, set your hope fully on the grace that will be brought to you at the revelation of Jesus Christ. As obedient children, do not be conformed to the passions of your former ignorance, but as he who called you is holy, you also be holy in all your conduct.* 1 Peter 1:13–15 (ESV)
>
> *[Paul said] Therefore I, the prisoner of the Lord, implore you to walk in a manner worthy of the calling with which you have been called, with all humility and gentleness, with patience, showing tolerance for one another in love, being diligent to preserve the unity of the Spirit in the bond of peace.* Ephesians 4:1–3 (NASB)

We live an abundant life through the gift of the Holy Spirit. Charles Spurgeon wrote that "an abundance of the Spirit brings the 'fullness of joy'". (Psalm 16:11) (KJV)

For the kingdom of God is not a matter of eating and drinking, but of righteousness, peace and joy in the Holy Spirit, because anyone who serves Christ in this way is pleasing to God and approved by men. Romans 14:17–18

May the God of hope fill you with all joy and peace as you trust in him, so that you may overflow with hope by the power of the Holy Spirit. Romans 15:13

We live abundantly when we live and claim His resurrection power and the all-powerful blood of the Lamb. Jesus has already won the victory for us and conquered death, paid the debt of our sins, foretold the end of the enemy, and shown us our inheritance. He has overcome the world for us. Jesus wins.

The thief comes only to steal and kill and destroy. I came that they may have life and have it abundantly. John 10:10 (ESV)

They overcame him by the blood of the Lamb and by the word of their testimony; they did not love their lives so much as to shrink from death. Revelation 12:11

But thanks be to God, who gives us the victory through our Lord Jesus Christ. 1 Corinthians 15:57 (ESV)

He is clothed with a robe dipped in blood, and His name is called The Word of God. And the armies in heaven, clothed in fine linen, white and clean, followed Him on white horses. Now out of His mouth goes a sharp sword, that with it he should strike the nations. And He Himself will rule them with a rod of iron. He Himself treads the winepress of the fierceness and wrath of Almighty God. And He has on His robe and on His thigh a name written: KING OF KINGS AND LORD OF LORDS. Revelation 19:14–16(NKJV)

...And the devil who had deceived them was thrown into the lake of fire and sulfur where the beast and the false prophet were, and they will be tormented day and night forever and ever. Revelation 20:10 (ESV)

For everyone that has been born of God overcomes the world. And this is the victory that has overcome the world—our faith. 1 *John 5:4 (ESV)*

We will produce fruits from the Holy Spirit when we live in Jesus' fulfillment, His victory. Claim Jesus' victory when praying for someone's salvation and ask God to surround this person with ministering Christians. Form a prayer group. Pray over areas to have a spiritual revival and the health of your children's schools. Pray for your church and pastor. Cry out to God that our country will turn back to Him. Pray for the peace of Israel. Pray without ceasing, ever knowing that God always hears our prayers. Speak life and truth in love over those that He puts in your path.

We will know God's good and perfect will when we stay in His Word and offer ourselves as a living sacrifice each day. Let's be *doers* of the Word. Commit each day to the Lord as you offer yourself to Him and enjoy His blessings that come from being in His presence and the privilege of being His servant, even when it's tough. Though we <u>will</u> have trials in this life, our hope and joy come from the Lord. In the midst of these trials our faith is increased and our relationship with Jesus is deepened to enjoy a more abundant life in Christ.

Jesus said, "I lay down my life for you." He was willing to give <u>all</u> to show us His love for us. Such love, such wondrous love. Fix your eyes on Jesus, the author and perfecter of our faith. Receive the joy of knowing that you will spend eternity with Jesus. Go forth in His love and kindness to show that Jesus is the way and the truth and the life. Hallelujah! Praise God! In Christ Jesus' love we remain.

"Do not be grieved, for the joy of the LORD is your strength." *Nehemiah 8:10b (NASB)*

Abide in me and I in you. John 15:4a (ESV)

As the Father has loved me, so have I loved you. Now remain in my love. If you obey my commands, you will remain in my love, just as I have obeyed my Father's commands and remain in his love. I have told you this so that my joy may be in you and that your joy may be complete. My command is this: Love each other as I have loved you. Greater love has no one than this, that he lay down his life for his friends. You are my friends if you do what I command. I no longer call you servants, because a servant does not know his master's business. Instead, I have called you friends, for everything that I learned from my Father I have made known to you. You did not choose me, but I chose you and appointed you to go and bear fruit—fruit that will last… John 15:9–16

And so begins our next journey to help fill His Kingdom. Jesus wants us to be fishers of men. He has a mission for each and every one of us. We will never be perfect. God knows the good, the bad, and the ugly in us all. If we are honest with Him and walk with Him, He will use us. By showing Jesus' love, we will shine His light in a world that is turning away from Him. Let's increase His Kingdom.

"Let your light so shine before men, that they may see your good works, and glorify your Father which is in heaven." Matthew 5:15 (KJV)

Jesus said to them again, "Peace be with you. As the Father has sent me, even so I am sending you." John 20:21 (ESV)

Journaling Exercise

1. Who can you lovingly lead to Christ through the power of the Holy Spirit? Pray for the Holy Spirit to guide you and to draw them in.

2. Please listen online to "Through All of It" by Colton Dixon to reflect on our journey to this point.

3. Please listen online to "Come Alive (Dry Bones)" by Lauren Daigle to inspire us to fill His Kingdom.

WEEK 10
GROUP QUESTIONS

1. List loved ones who need prayer in their suffering. Use the prayer for suffering in lesson 36 and insert all of the names that are on the list.

2. Does anyone have a testimony of healing?

3. List the names of those who you know are going through persecution.

4. Say the prayer of persecution in Lesson 37 and insert all of the names on your list. Remember the Christians around the world being persecuted unto death.

5. Who is the "new man"?

6. Pray for the peace of Israel. All blessings come through them. Pray for wisdom for our leaders to support Israel.

7. Discuss the similarities of Jesus' return in Matthew 24, Mark 13 and Luke 22.

8. As a group, pray for the salvation of loved ones, areas that need to be prayed over, and whomever God puts on your heart.

AUTHOR NOTE

Be encouraged that God knows that while we walk this earth there is a constant struggle with the enemy, the world, and our flesh. God loves us unconditionally in this battle and always wants what is best for us. Realize that worry, doubt, fear, and rebellion are not from God. Jesus' ways are the complete opposite of this battle in our mind. When you have this struggle, do what you are resisting anyway. Don't let condemnation and feeling defeated win. Call your thoughts captive to Jesus and revert back to His love. Jesus performs miracles in this realm.

We are all sinners saved by grace. It is a battle out there. God keeps reminding us that the battle is His. We just have to repent, have faith, and be brave. When I told God that I wasn't brave enough to do what He was calling me to do, the answer came from the Holy Spirit in the song below, "You Make Me Brave." Praise God, Jesus will make us brave.

In repentance and rest is your salvation, in quietness and trust is your strength. Isaiah 30:15b

"Have I not commanded you? Be strong and courageous. Do not be terrified; do not be discouraged, for the LORD your God will be with you wherever you go." *Joshua 1:9*

Two last songs to listen to: "You Make Me Brave" by Amanda Cook & Bethel Music and "Ever Be" by Aaron Shust.

QUICK REFERENCE PRAYERS

A Nightly Prayer to Sleep in Peace

Heavenly Father, we thank you for all the blessings in our lives. (Tell Him what you are thankful for. Pray for those who need prayer.)

Lord Jesus, please fill this home with the light of Your presence. You are the Light of the World and where Your light is, there can be no darkness. I plead the blood of Jesus over this home as an umbrella of protection. I call on You, Jesus, to send down warring angels to guard and protect our doors so that no evil may enter and only good dwells within this home. I claim this house as a house of the LORD.

Jesus, please heal us with Your touch and restore our bodies as we sleep and keep us free from pain. Father, please place us under Your wing and give us dreams only from Jesus and words from the Holy Spirit. I pray that the peace of the LORD be upon each one of us and guard our hearts and minds in Christ Jesus throughout the night. You will keep in perfect peace him whose mind is steadfast, because he trusts in You. We trust You, LORD. In Jesus' precious name we pray, amen.

A Daily Prayer for Doing God's Work

Heavenly Father, I pray the armor of God on so that I may stand firm. I pray the Helmet of Salvation and the Breastplate of Righteousness secure on my chest. Gird my loins with the Truth and shod my feet with the Preparation of the Gospel of Peace. In one hand I wield the Shield of Faith to resist all fiery darts of the enemy, and the other the Sword of the Spirit which is the Word of God, sharper than any two-edged sword. In Jesus' name I pray the armor of God on and plead the blood of Jesus over me for protection. I loose anything not from Jesus and I bind all my thoughts captive to the obedience of Jesus Christ. God did not give me a spirit of fear, but power, love, and a sound mind.

I thank you, Father, for allowing me to be Your child and I am so grateful that You love me and will always be there for me. Please examine my heart and if anything is displeasing to You or if there is anyone I need to forgive, show me so that I may repent. [pause and repent]

Heavenly Father, I offer my body today as a living sacrifice to do Your good and perfect will. May I be a vessel for You to use for holy works. I pray for spiritual wisdom and revelation from You, LORD. I ask that my thoughts be Your thoughts and my words be Your words. Please close my mouth to what I am not supposed to say. May the words of my mouth and meditation of my heart be pleasing in Your sight and may I glorify You, LORD.

I die to myself today and live for You, Jesus. I am not my own, but was bought at a great price. I claim the victory of this day, because You have already overcome the world for us. Please shine Your light through me, Jesus. Give me Your eyes to see people as You see them and Your heart to love them as You love them. Fill me with Your grace.

Holy Spirit, You are welcome here and I ask that You be present in me and give me utterance.

This is the day the LORD has made, let us rejoice and be glad! I pray this all in Jesus' precious name, amen.

A Prayer to Serve

Lord Jesus, anoint my head with Your oil of joy until my cup overflows with Your grace. For it is by Your grace I have been saved and by Your grace I have been forgiven much. Please break my heart, Lord, for what breaks Yours and give me Your eyes to see them as you see them. May I be able to extend Your love and grace today. In the precious name of Jesus I pray, amen.

Prayer Against Condemnation

*Heavenly Father, I declare in the name of Jesus that my righteous standing comes from Jesus Christ. As He is, which is at the right hand of God and full of righteousness, so am I in this world. Thank you LORD for giving me Your Spirit within me that is greater than he who is in the world. It is written, "For you did not receive a spirit that makes you a slave again to fear, but you received the Spirit of sonship." I claim my inheritance as a son/daughter of God that sits at Your table and I am a co-heir with Christ, **so get behind me, Satan**.*

There is no condemnation for those that are in Christ Jesus. I loose any power the devil has over my mind and I bind my mind to the obedience of Jesus Christ. As it is written, whatever is loosed on earth is loosed in heaven, and whatever is bound on earth is bound in heaven.

I can do all things through Christ who strengthens me. I plead the blood of Jesus over me and ask for the peace of God, a peace that surpasses all understanding and guards my heart and mind in Christ Jesus. I surrender all to You, Jesus. In Your Holy Name I pray, amen.

A Prayer to Combat the Enemy

*Heavenly Father, I praise Your Holy Name. Thank you for sending down Your precious Son to shine His light and show us the truth of Your Word. **I claim the power of the light of Jesus to be present throughout this house** [wherever you are]. Where there is Your light, there can be no darkness.*

Jesus, your perfect love casts out all fear. Fear has to do with punishment and You have taken ALL the punishment that I deserve. You said, "It is finished." I praise and thank you for Your perfect love on the cross! God placed You in the highest place and gave You the name that is above all names, and at the name of Jesus, all knees should bow, in heaven and on earth and under the earth, and every tongue confess that Jesus is Lord.

God did not give me a spirit of fear but of power, love, and a sound mind. I claim Your power and Your love over my mind and I call all my thoughts captive to the obedience of Jesus Christ.

Your Word is sharper than a two-edged sword, able to separate the joints from the marrow, and I claim Your words that "no weapon formed against me shall prosper." We were purchased for God at a price, by the precious blood of Jesus Christ. **I claim the power of the blood of Jesus over me** and ask for You, Jesus, to send down warring angels to surround me and keep me safe. In Jesus' Mighty Name I pray, amen.

Prayer of Faith

Heavenly Father, I pray for the faith of Abraham. His faith was so strong that he was willing to sacrifice his own son in obedience to You. I struggle at times to give my whole heart, trusting that You are in control. Please help my unbelief so that my faith is pure and unshaken. Jesus said in Mark 9:23 that "everything is possible for him who believes." To this, the father of the possessed boy responded, "Lord, I believe, help my unbelief."

Lord, I believe, help my unbelief. Help me to increase my faith and trust in You.

Help me to understand that all I need to do is fix my eyes on You, Jesus, for as it is written, You alone are "the author and perfecter of our faith" (Hebrews 12:2). Please fill me with your love.

Thank you for Your goodness, Thank you for Your grace. In Jesus' mighty name I pray, amen.

A Prayer for an Anxious Heart

Heavenly Father, Thank you for Your great mercy. I come before You with an anxious heart. In 1 John 5 You reveal that I have the confidence to approach You and if I ask anything that is in accordance to Your will, You hear me. And if I know that You hear me, whatever I ask, I know that I will have what I ask of You.

When Jesus raised Lazarus from the dead, He said, "Father, I thank you that You have heard me." (Tell God what you are anxious about.)

Father, I thank you that You have heard me. This battle is Yours, LORD. I put these issues into Your loving hands. Jesus, I ask You to calm this raging sea in me. You are in control and it is well with my soul. In Jesus' Holy Name I pray, amen.

Prayer for Revelation

Heavenly Father, Creator of the heavens and the earth, Maker of us all, I praise Your Almighty Name. You parted the sea. You command the eagle to fly. You are the source of *all wisdom. Your ways are higher than mine and Your thoughts are higher than mine and I seek to know Your will, LORD, not mine. I ask that You give me spiritual wisdom and revelation to hear Your will. Holy Spirit, please be present in me and speak to me.*

Abba, I cry out to you. I seek your face, O LORD. I want to know You more. I want to feel You more. You knew me before I was even born and I want whatever Your plan is for my life. I love you LORD and thank you that You first loved me. In Jeremiah 6:16, You say to "stand at the crossroads and look; ask for the ancient paths, ask where the good way is and walk in it, and you will find rest for your souls."

LORD, I need revelation of _____. I ask that You show me the ancient paths and where the good way is. I desire Your path of righteousness.

In Jesus' precious name I pray, amen.

Prayer of Intercession against Spiritual Warfare

Holy, Holy, Holy, is the Lord God Almighty; we praise Your Great Name.

Heavenly Father, because we have a high priest that sits at Your right hand that was perfectly blameless and died for us, we have the confidence to approach the throne of grace and ask to receive mercy for_____. Father, we thank you that You always hear our prayers. We stand in the gap for _____ with our faith.

Your Word is living and active and sharper than any two-edged sword, able to separate the soul and the spirit and the joints from the marrow. We claim the power of Your Word over this prayer. It is written that the "fervent, effectual prayer of a righteous man availeth much, and we ask that You hear our petitions and have mercy on_____.

We lift up _____ to Your throne and ask that You hide_____ in the secret place of the Most High and allow_____ to rest under the shadow of the Almighty. Protect _____ under Your wings where ____ may find refuge.

The book of Revelation tells us that the enemy was overcome by the blood of the Lamb. Jesus, you have delivered us from the power of darkness with Your blood. We plead the precious blood of Jesus poured over _____. We claim Your mighty resurrection power to be upon _____ and we ask that a hedge of protection be also placed around_____. You are the light that brought light to us all and we ask that Your light surround and engulf_____. Where Your light is, Jesus, there can be no darkness.

At the name of Jesus every knee should bow, of things in heaven, and things on earth, and things under the earth. We claim the power of Your Mighty Name over all principalities of darkness that come against ____ and that no weapon formed against ____shall prosper.

Perfect love casts out all fear. We claim Your perfect love over _____, Jesus. We ask that all ____ thoughts be held captive to the obedience of Jesus Christ. May the peace of the Lord be upon ____, a peace that surpasses all understanding and guards our hearts and minds in Christ Jesus.

Jesus, please send down mighty warrior angels to guard and protect _____. "If God is for us, who can be against us?" We thank you LORD for Your promises and we praise Your Mighty Name. We pray this all in the precious name of Jesus, amen.

Prayer for Persecution (substitute name, he/she and him/her)

Heavenly Father, we praise You for Your loving kindness and we ask that we can come before You and lift _____ to Your throne and that You grant Your great mercy. _____ has suffered for doing good and, as it is written, this is commendable to the Lord. Those who wish to harm _____ surround ____, and we ask that, like Daniel, the mouths of these lions are shut. We stand firm in our faith and claim Your words that 'no weapon that is formed against ____ shall prosper and every tongue that accuses____ in judgment You will condemn'. This is our heritage that You promise.

God we know that You hate injustice and iniquity. We ask for Your justice to prevail. You say in 1 Chronicles, "Beware, lest you touch my anointed," and in Deuteronomy You tell us that "It is mine to avenge; I will repay." Thank you for these promises.

Please grant favor to _____ in the eyes of those that oppose____. We claim Your promise that those of Yours that have been shamed or disgraced shall inherit a double portion. We rejoice that You tell us that "If God is for you, who can be against you!" And that "The LORD is with me; I will not be afraid, what can man do to me?"

We trust you, LORD, and we give You this battle, for as it is written, 'the battle is the Lord's'. We commit this situation to You. Lead us to victory.

In Lamentations it is written: "Because of the LORD'S great love we are not consumed, for his compassions never fail. They are new every morning; great is your faithfulness."

Thank you, Father, for great is Your faithfulness. In Your Almighty Son's name we pray, amen.

Example of a Prayer for Healing Sickness (lay hands on the area of pain)
*Heavenly Father, we praise You and thank you for Your great love and mercy. Lord Jesus, You are Emmanuel, God with us, and You comfort us and heal us. When You walked this earth You healed the sick of their afflictions, and You still do. The woman who bled for 12 years knew if she just touched Your garment then she would be healed. We ask to touch the tassels of your garment and be healed. By her faith she was healed. The blind beggar asked for mercy and to be healed of his blindness. By his faith You healed him. We stand firm in our faith and we ask You, Jesus, son of David, for Your mercy and for _____ to be miraculously healed. You said that this sign shall accompany those who believe, that they can "place their hands on sick people, and they will get well." In the name of Jesus Christ, **be healed**. We ask to loose this spirit of infirmity. Loose any sorrow, illness, and pain that is not from You, and bind it to the healing love from You, Jesus.*

In Deuteronomy it is written that the diseases of Egypt shall not touch Your people and in Revelation it is written that the enemy was overcome by the blood of the Lamb. In the name of Jesus Christ of Nazareth, we claim Your resurrection power and Your blood poured over_____ to overcome this illness and by Your stripes they are healed.

May the will of our Father be done and the peace of the LORD be upon _____. In Jesus' precious name we pray, amen.

Keep your hands on the area of pain and praise and thank God.

"Holy, holy, holy is the Lord God Almighty, who was, and is, and is to come." *Revelation 4:8b*

A free eBook edition is available with the purchase of this book.

To claim your free eBook edition:

1. Download the Shelfie app.
2. Write your name in upper case in the box.
3. Use the Shelfie app to submit a photo.
4. Download your eBook to any device.

Shelfie

A free eBook edition is available
with the purchase of this print book.

CLEARLY PRINT YOUR NAME ABOVE IN UPPER CASE

Instructions to claim your free eBook edition:
1. Download the Shelfie app for Android or iOS
2. Write your name in **UPPER CASE** above
3. Use the Shelfie app to submit a photo
4. Download your eBook to any device

Print & Digital Together Forever.

Snap a photo

Free eBook

Read anywhere

Printed in the USA
CPSIA information can be obtained
at www.ICGtesting.com
JSHW022213140824
68134JS00018B/1037